The Future as the Presence of Shared Hope

The essays in this volume were presented at the John XXIII Institute theology symposium, on the theme The Future as the Presence of Shared Hope, held at Saint Xavier College, Chicago, on October 27-29, 1967.

The Future
as the Presence
of Shared Hope

edited with an Introduction by
MARYELLEN MUCKENHIRN

SHEED AND WARD : NEW YORK

Contents

The Future as the Presence of Shared Hope

MARYELLEN MUCKENHIRN

Introduction

WIDELY DIFFERING PERSPECTIVES on a single theme indicate that the theme itself is not only open-ended but in a state of intellectual ferment. Such is the theme of this book. It deals with one of the most creative areas in contemporary theology and philosophy, an area increasingly to the fore in writing, lecturing, and symposia titles. There are many reasons for the present interest in the topic of the future, ranging from questions about economic and political planning to the deepest searching of man for the meaning of his very existence. The unity underlying the essays of this book comes from the theme of the future precisely as it raises speculative questions for philosophers and theologians, those whose profession it is to reflect on the meaning of life and human values.

It seems important to make a few comments about the words "eschatology" and "future." They are not considered to be synonymous by many contemporary thinkers. The traditional scholastic theology used "eschatology" to describe the section of content which dealt with the "last things," the truths held by faith about death, judgment, hell, and heaven. There have always been many difficulties with this section of theology

because the realities described were, for the one doing the
reflecting, objects neither of personal experience nor of human
communal past history in the same sense as the great saving
events which were believed as already accomplished by God in
history. Thus traditional eschatology has tended to seem un-
real at best, and highly imaginative at worst.

Scripture scholars, on the other hand, have used "eschatological" to refer to biblical passages which refer to the future in
different literary or time senses. Exegesis of such passages
differs greatly and has produced varying interpretations. There
is a wide range of disagreement among professional scripture
scholars at present. This is especially true of the meaning of
passages dealing with events once future, now past, as contrasted with passages concerning events still future and even
trans-temporal.

The word "future" is at once so familiar and yet so mysterious that its usages vary greatly, depending on how a person
thinks and feels about events and realities which have not yet
occurred. The existential thrust of the future plays its part in
every instant of every human being's awareness of his own
reality. To be human is precisely to be aware of oneself as
changing, moving out of a past and into a future as yet un-
lived, of existing in a present which is an ever moving "now."
The writers in this book all opt for a future which is fundamentally one of hope, of positive expectation of some as yet
unpossessed good for man. There are other options, but they
lie outside the scope of the present work. Man's present
awareness of his future is here taken as one of hope, and of a
hope that is lived out and shared with others.

It will be obvious from the following essays that the topic of
the future is not only of interest to every human being in a

general way. It is today of special interest in academic speculation among philosophers and theologians. How does one speak meaningfully of what has not yet occurred? What is this future to which all of Judaeo-Christian revelation and history seems to be related? What sort of language suits reflection on realities which have already happened and yet are not completed?

The current upheaval in such professional thinking is due to a convergence of scientific biblical studies, contemporary philosophical phenomenology, social psychology and the constantly deepening awareness of the mystery of the human person. These forces, coupled with the newness of the twentieth-century human experience of existence in a technologized world and within a web of instant communication, are only some of the elements at work in the present vital rethinking of the meaning of human life and its relation to what men have called Christianity. Each of these aspects raises questions of language in the sense of meaningful ways of communicating today with persons who live today. The contemporary experience is so new and so constantly developing that many persons simply do not comprehend a theological or philosophical language forged out of different and earlier human life experience.

It is within the awareness of this contemporary language problem in religious thought that the following essays are particularly valuable. The seven writers speak to the theme of the future as the presence of shared hope with varying manners of expression. Five of the authors reflect from an opening assent of religious faith in a revealing God. Dr. Rylaarsdam and Rabbi Borowitz both bring special insight to the Hebrew scriptures. The former shows convincingly the need to read the Christian scriptures in the light of the earlier writings. Rabbi

Borowitz shares the belief and hope of a man who lives today out of the vitality of the Jewish sacred writings as well as their communal awareness. Father Crossan speaks the professional language of the scientific exegete of contemporary scripture research. Dr. Moltmann brings to the topic a critical discourse on the new and inclusive principle of hope, drawn out of his study of Hegel, Marx, and Bloch. Dr. Gilkey addresses the reader as a creative theologian aware of both the history of doctrine and the impact of contemporary cultural values.

The two remaining authors philosophize from their own reflection on their human existence in today's world. While opting personally for belief in God, they do not start their professional search from this premise. Dr. Schaldenbrand works within the European personalist tradition of Gabriel Marcel and Paul Ricoeur. Father Burrell takes a more linguistic and epistemological approach, highly influenced by Bernard Lonergan. It seems legitimate to expect that vital theologizing will tend to move into language patterns at present represented by such contemporary modes of reflection. Of course there are other language options not represented here at all.

Having pointed out the differences among the writers in modes of expression, we can now note several important underlying premises accepted by all of them in their essays. The first is their agreement about the importance of this theme of the future for contemporary study. The currents of despair, the existence of terrible human suffering, a seemingly uncontrollable fascination with power and violence are only too evident in our world. Without hope, how does one live? But for what kind of future does one hope, based on what assurances? No answers will be considered meaningful that are unrelated to the improvement of human life here on earth, or that refuse to face up to the agonizing questions raised by life as we experience it. As man's sense of his power to make the future increases, his sense of its unknowableness can overwhelm him. No topic is more urgent, difficult or profound for those who care whether they and their fellow men can continue to hope today.

The writers also agree that hope is a human reality in one's life which depends on sharing life and its desires and actions with others. Some address themselves more directly than others to this corporate aspect. But none would hold that the individual can survive without a sense of being part of the larger human family, of belonging personally to some specific group within it. Note here the tragic connection in modern thought between alienation and despair. This shared quality of hope raises again and on another level the earlier point about languages for meaningful communication today.

Another point presumed by the authors is that the very nature of man demands that he be related to some transcendent reality. Man is a living relationship to others, and finally to some ultimate Other. These statements would be acceptable to the writers, though their personally expanded statements of meaning would surely range as widely as the chapters at hand. The main point here is that there is no position of total closure to transcendence among these chapters, as for example that of the atheistic humanist. Dialogue with persons of such persuasion is crucial, but the present chapters deal with the theme only within the presupposition of a transcendent being beyond man.

A final quality common to all the authors is that they are interested in a type of reflection on the future and on hope which not only illuminates the present, but also does something in the present to bring about the desired future. They are non-escapist and non-utopian. They see the human future, whatever its shape, as the result of human choices and effort, not as a product of vague forces or mere passage of time.

The present chapters of this book were once only future projects. They came from a shared hope in the value of thinking and reflecting and growing through common experiences. It seems interesting to note that our usage of "presented" would make it possible to say that these chapters were "present-ed," made present for hearing and discussion, at the John XXIII Institute symposium. But they are here "presented" for the general reader and student, who in the future will share these ideas about hope. Such sharing already makes a reality of the future toward which hope points the heart of man.

JÜRGEN MOLTMANN

"Behold, I make all things new": The Category of the New in Christian Theology

JÜRGEN MOLTMANN, a brilliant figure among younger European theologians, has been called "the theologian of hope." He speaks to the topic "The Category of the New in Christian Theology" out of a profound understanding of the interweaving of church and world, of theology and philosophy.

His first academic appointment came in 1958 as Professor of Systematic Theology and History of Theology at Wuppertal. Subsequently, he held posts at Bonn University and is currently at Tübingen University. During the 1967-68 academic year he was visiting professor at Duke University, North Carolina.

Dr. Moltmann is co-editor of *Evangelische Theologie, Verkündigung und Forschung,* and *Begegnung mit Polen.* He is a member of the Synode der Evangelischen Kirche in Deutschland, of the Marxismum-Kommission, of the Oekumenische Arbeitskreis, and of the Paulus-Gesellschaft.

In addition to *The Theology of Hope* (New York: Harper and Row, 1967), a second work is now available in English: *Two Studies in the Theology of Bonhoeffer,* with Jürgen Weissbach (New York: Scribner's, 1967).

In German, he has published numerous articles and essays in *Evangelische Theologie, Verkündigung und Forschung, Monatsschrift fur Pastoraltheologie, Zeitschrift fur Kirchengeschichte, Markur, Concilium, Communio Viatorum.* He is author of *Christoph Pezel und der Calvinism in Bremen,* 1957; and *Predestination und Perseveranz,* 1961. Dr. Moltmann is also editor of *Calvin Studien,* 1959, and of *Anfänge dialektischer Theologie,* I, II, 1963.

I. Where Is the "New" in Christianity?

"Nothing new happens under the sun," says Ecclesiastes. "Hence all is vanity." In saying this he expressed that wisdom of resignation which can make man melancholy in his serenity. But if there can be nothing new in the world, it means that there is no real future. And if there is no future, there is no real history. If there is no history, our world is not open, but shut in, and man, too, is not a being who is open and full of questions and hopes for the future, but one who is enclosed and imprisoned in himself.

If we consider our contemporary situation, we find that in all areas of life the special feature of modern times is that everywhere we are asking for something that is "new." The modern world is modern precisely because men are fascinated by the prospects of a future which so far has not taken place anywhere, and hence will be new. This is true everywhere except in the church. Here hardly anything new happens, and if we do carry out reforms, it is always with the fear that we may thereby be losing what is best. In the church, above all other places, men are conservative, attached to the past. At a time when everything is changing and undergoing renewal, there seems to be an unconscious desire here, in the religious sphere, to preserve a place for continuity, tradition and the element of changelessness. God is invoked not as the power of the new, who creates the world's future, but as the power of eternity and everlastingness in the face of anxiety for the future.

Greek philosophy did not make the category of the *novum* a specific theme of its reflections. Plato and Aristotle make only passing reference to this concept. The *novum* is for them neither a category for grasping history and the future ontologically nor a category for positing the openness of human existence anthropologically.

If we take up the basic writings of Christianity, we find not a homogeneous document of revelation, but an antithesis between "Old" and "New" Testaments. Obviously, therefore, Christianity is a matter of tension and conflict between "old" and "new." Now how can we have such an origin without that conflict yielding a historical consciousness which seeks the "new" rather than the "old"? If we take up the New Testament, on practically every page we meet the word "new" —new heaven and a new earth, the new Jerusalem, the new wine, the new song, the new name, and finally the gathering up of everything new into the future of God, who says at the end: "Behold, I make all things new." The new (*kainos, novum*) is here the essence of the wholly other, the factor of surprise which the messianic future brings. In the midst of the life which has become old, hope is roused by the new. The new creation is the goal of this hope, and Christian hope recognizes that through Christ's resurrection from the dead this new future has become already present and effective for every being in pain. With Easter the future of God's new world shines into the present situation of the old world and "into the sufferings of this time." Through this new element believers recognize themselves. For in Christ a new people of God, a new man—yes, a new humanity—is formed of Jew and Gentile. The proclamation takes place in new tongues. Life is placed under the new commandment of love. Through faith and baptism man becomes a new creature. A new obedience fills his life.

Even from this quite superficial survey of the use of the word "new," the extent to which God, the future and the new are joined together in the thought of the New Testament is clear. God is the dynamism of the future and is believed in as the creator of a new world. Out of this future, new energy already forces its way into the present, so that man can find rebirth and renewal, repentance and social change. We are confronted here with an eschatologically oriented faith. It is not concerned with an event that took place at the beginning of time nor with explaining why the world exists and why it is as it is. It is oriented to a new future, and hence its object is to change the world rather than explain it, to alter human existence rather than elucidate it. This eschatological attitude towards the world is concerned more with making history than with interpreting nature. For the history we are discussing is the sphere in which something that is new, that has not heretofore taken place, comes into being.

This brief survey is by way of explanation of the light in which we are viewing the New Testament—as the "testament of the new" and the new covenant in Jesus Christ, as man's covenant with the new situation God promises and will create. The category of the *novum* does not detract from our concept of God. In Deutero-Isaiah *bara* signifies not so much creation out of nothing as God's power to create the new out of the old.

If this is true, then we can break into lamentation over the condition of the church in our own day. Since the beginning of modern times the center of humanity's hopes for something new from God has been moving away from the church, and man's spiritual energies have become channeled into revolutions and urgent social change. It was the forces of reaction and conservatism that remained behind in the church. Thus the Christian church became confined to the "religious" dimension. She cultivated tradition. Her authority was justified by what had been in force always and everywhere from the earliest times.

The modern world, on the other hand, thinks in a revolutionary fashion of the future and looks for the new things which now become possible. In religious tradition men become the recipients of an old message. In the modern world they become pioneers of progress, trailblazers of the future and discoverers of new possibilities. The church lives on memories, the world on hopes. In theology one proves the truth by quotations from the Fathers; in the modern world, by the success of experiments. We shall put an end to this schism only if Christianity achieves a rebirth in terms of its origin in the "Testament of the new."

Now it is not true that new hope comes from forgetting the past. Hope too has its memory; it recalls that past history in which the promises for the future were heard and in which the dawn of a new creation began to appear. Such "remembrance" is not a "remembrance of things past" in Marcel Proust's sense but is fidelity to hope. "May my right arm wither if I should forget you . . . Jerusalem." We remember what has been promised but has not yet taken place; we recall the claim of the past on the future. Wherever in history everything appears already achieved, already completed, this sort of memory has no place. History forces itself on the present only to the extent that it has not yet been achieved, in connection with some past event, clearly full of promise, whose possibilities have not yet developed. It is in this sense that we now turn back to ask about the basis of a future which is in store for us today, so that we may lay hold of it today. The new is never totally new. It is always preceded by a dream, a promise, an anticipation. "He who does not hope for what is beyond expectation will not find it" (Heraclitus).

II. The Prophecy of the New

In Israel Yahweh was known through the stories of the patriarchs, the Exodus, the making of the Covenant and the entrance into the Promised Land. Hence, to trust in Yahweh meant to remember the history of his promises and their fulfillments and to identify oneself with the Exodus generation. "In every generation man is obliged to think of himself as having taken part in the movement out of Egypt" (Mishna Pesachim X,5). But when, in the great wars of destruction from the eighth to the sixth century, Israel's unity was destroyed and her very existence threatened, Israel fell out with the God of her history. Prophet rose against prophet. In the face of imminent annihilation there were prophets who asserted that Zion must not fall, for "here is the temple of the Lord." His name dwelt in his temple, and his presence, his power and his fidelity were guaranteed by his name. But the great prophets of doom rose up and proclaimed the coming destruction as a new, unexpected action of God with respect to his disobedient people. For God is not only a "God close by" but also a "God approaching from afar." Israel has broken the old covenant with God. Hence God is no longer bound by it. True, he judges his people according to the law of the covenant, but in this judgment the covenant itself seems to collapse. The God of history, known from the past through remembrance, becomes for Israel a hidden God. Therefore the prophets proclaim that with God's judgment of his people a new act of God is heralded and will come.

The prophets go on interpreting the old traditions of Yahweh. Yet, as they confront these traditions, they bring to expression something new. A future is to come from God which, even considered over against these old traditions, is new. The "God of history" is changing into the "God of the future." While Hosea stands in the Exodus-tradition, Isaiah is aware only of the David- and the Zion-tradition. With Jeremiah, Ezechiel and finally Deutero-Isaiah the old Desert-tradition comes once again to the fore. Nevertheless, the relationship of these prophets to their traditions is ruptured. The coming judgment puts an end to the order of Israel's existence up to this point. The guarantees contained in the traditions of election are annulled by Israel's guilt. The only thing Israel can hold onto is Yahweh's new act in history which the prophets proclaim. Thus for Israel the basis of salvation shifts from the past into the future. Israel's faith changes from a living remembrance into a living hope. The old dogmas of salvation history lose their actuality, since Israel's life and death are now being decided in terms of what is to come. In this Gerhard von Rad has rightly seen the hour of birth for biblical eschatology.

But how do the prophets proclaim the new thing which is coming? They do not believe in a new God; hence they link the new reality which God will create with the memory of his fidelity. Thus Hosea predicts a "new occupation of the land," Isaiah a "new David," Jeremiah a "new covenant" and Deutero-Isaiah a "new exodus." With Isaiah the old salvation history still has so much force that it can be presupposed as the basis of God's new actions. For Deutero-Isaiah, however, the change has become so deep that he hears God commanding: "Remember not the former things, nor consider the things of old. Behold, I am doing a new thing: now it springs forth, do you not perceive it?" (Is. 43:18, 19).[1] This does not mean that Israel as the Israel of God no longer exists. On the contrary, Israel has learned, through the voices of the prophets, to understand its catastrophes as the judgments of the same God who called Israel into being. Israel survived because it could recognize God's faithfulness in his judgment, and thus continued to adhere to him. In the discontinuity of history Israel found its own continuity in the faithfulness of God. Therefore we can understand the Old Testament prophecy of the New as a new act in the history of God's promises.

From this prophecy of the new we can learn three things: (1) The new is proclaimed in judgment over the old. God kills and brings to life. The new is preceded by the destruction of the old—that in which guilt has been incurred—and not by the development or evolution of the old. It is not out of the possibilities one has, but in the impossible situation with which one is faced, that the new shows itself as God's creative act. God's new reality is always a *novum ex nihilo*. When all hopes have died, there comes the wave of the future like a spirit of resurrection into the dead bones (Ezechiel 37). (2) The first anticipation of the new future always takes the form of a recourse to the analogies of history. In the images of the "new Zion," the "new exodus" and the "new occupation of the land" the new is pictured as a renewal of the origin from which one has fallen away. But in fact, as Gershom Scholem observes, the images of the new Jerusalem always convey more than ever took place in the case of the old Jerusalem. The new is more than the restitution of the old, since through guilt and judgment something has intervened which cannot simply be undone. (3) This recourse to the analogies of history in order to understand the new reality of the future brings history back to life again. What once was is now past, and has its force only as a type and an anticipation of the new.[2] Thus out of the past emerges a promise of what is to come. One no longer sees in the past a mass of finished events; these events, which appear to be over and done with, become real anticipations of the future. Thereby past history is understood as a promise of the future still to come. We see that clearly in Deutero-Isaiah. He understands his own present message not as mere promise, but as a gospel: "How beautiful upon the mountains are the feet of him who brings good tidings. . . . , who publishes salvation" (52.7). Here the word we translate as "gospel" appears for the first time in the Bible. It is not only an announcement of salvation (*Heilsankündigung*) but an offer of salvation (*Heilszusage*). It is not a statement about a distant future, but is the presence of this future in Word.

III. The Apostolate of the New

Easter is the day of birth for the Christian church. Yet, faced with this event in which the crucified Christ had once more appeared to them, all the first Christian communities found it an enigma. These Easter appearances of Christ called forth a limitless astonishment and an open questioning. Who is this person who has been crucified and raised from the dead? (At this point I take up the interpretation offered by Ernst Käsemann in his New Testament studies.) At first, patterns from Israel's tradition, namely the faith in a Messiah (Son of David) and the apocalyptic expectation of the Son of Man, suggested themselves. Hence the first Jewish-Christian community gathered around Peter saw in the risen one the Son of David, the hidden Messiah of Israel and—above and beyond that—the hidden Son of Man. Consequently the community understood itself, under the leadership of the twelve apostles, as the "renewed people of the twelve tribes" and as the Christian synagogue. Hence it remained within the "pale of Israel," maintaining the law and circumcision. No grounds were found for a mission to the Gentiles. God would call the Gentiles only when Zion was restored. This community, therefore, grasped the new reality which Christ brought only in terms of their remembrance of Israel's history and hopes.

Another understanding of the new situation brought about by the First Easter developed later, beginning probably within the circle of the seven gathered about Stephen. They applied to themselves the apocalyptic prediction that the temple would be destroyed, and a new temple, not built by men, would come. Hence they were persecuted. Moving on to Antioch, they encountered the surprising fact that the Spirit of Christ was being bestowed on the Gentiles, who were becoming believers without having been Jews. At this point it became evident that Christ could no longer be considered merely Israel's Messiah; he was also the Lord of the Gentiles.

Thus a new community comprising Jews and Gentiles comes into being in which the former distinctions are no longer maintained. This community can no longer call itself the old people of God "renewed." It interprets itself rather as "the new people of God" and adopts the organizational expression *ecclesia* as a name. Thus the memory link with Israel's history is nearly cut. Something completely new becomes reality. Hence the gospel of this community runs: "Here there cannot be Greek and Jew, circumcised and uncircumcised, barbarian, Scythian, slave, free man, but Christ is all, and in all" (Col. 3:11). They thereby proclaim "Spirit and freedom" in the whole world. As the Corinthian community understands it, "The Lord is the Spirit." For them freedom means leaving all obligations of the law, society, and the body. For them Spirit is the supra-earthly sphere of heaven. Whoever believes is already risen. But thereby the remembrance of Jesus and his cross on earth is lost among these enthusiastic Corinthians. The Spirit assumes his place.

Yet another insight into the new situation brought by Christ is found in Paul. He knows the universal scope of the Hellenistic Christian faith. But as a Jew he nevertheless retains the realism of the Old Testament hope, which can never be satisfied with an inner, spiritual fulfillment of the promises. For him, then, the new reality which has appeared with Christ is a new creation of God. In order to say what is, properly speaking, new he goes beyond Israel's remembrance of history. The resurrection of Christ is an astounding miracle. There is nothing at all to compare it with, except the world's creation out of nothing. It is the God who calls non-being into being and raises the dead who has acted here in the case of Jesus (Rom. 4:17). Thus this future brought by Christ involves not the spiritualizing of man in an inner freedom, but the totally new creation of man and the world. What faith, Spirit and joy do above all is herald the greater things still to come in the world. By the new obedience of believers in the everyday life of this wretched world the resurrection of the body is anticipated. Here and now the future of this new creation is present only in Christ's cross and with those who become disciples of the crucified one. Thus with Paul the category of the new is understood more radically than by the prophets. The new is not a mere renewal, but the entrance of the wholly unexpected (1 Cor.2:7). The new thing of the future does not appear in the fact that the present is confirmed, nor in some correspondence to the good times of old, nor even in the restoration of the original creation. "The old has passed away, behold, the new has come" (2 Cor. 5:17). It is not out of the good factors which are at hand that God creates his new future, but out of the bad, the evil and the godless that he creates the new. God has chosen what is foolish in the eyes of the world; he has chosen what is weak and good for nothing (1 Cor. 1:27ff.). ". . . God chose what is low and despised in the world, even things that are not, to bring to nothing things that are" (28). As the God of the forsaken he enters, in revolutionary fashion, a world where all take pride in themselves. He exalts the humble and puts down the mighty from their seat (Luke 1:52). Is there thus for Paul no continuity between history and this new future? Yes, even for him there is continuity. But it does not consist in some human or immanent factor which is kept going; it is rather the fidelity of God, who, in creating the new, remembers and restores the old which has turned away from him and been lost. The expression "resurrection of the dead" means that God brings back the dead in his new creation and gathers up the lost. The new creation takes up, therefore, the old creation in itself. Continuity is established by the future, just as all historical continuity is created by the future which takes up into itself what has been lost. Thus historical continuity distinguishes itself in principle from organic or ontological continuity.

IV. Marcion and the Destruction of the New in Christianity

In an age which saw the rise of early Catholicism, Marcion, the most radical disciple of Paul, attempted once more to renew the church. The only work we know he wrote is titled *Antitheses*. From him comes the expression "New Testament" and the collection of Paul's letters. While the church of his time took the Old Testament as its Bible, it was through Marcion that what we still call the "New Testament" came into circulation. It was directed antithetically against the Old Testament. It was only after Marcion's time that the church made the one canon out of both. If we recognize this, we are more able to grasp the fact that this one canon comprising the Old and New Testaments contains dynamite. Marcion's *Antitheses* begins with the cry of astonished exultation: "O miracle beyond miracle, rapture, power and astonishment is it that one can say nothing at all about the gospel or compare it with anything at all!" For Marcion the new order which Christ brings is without analogy. Everything which existed hitherto and which one knew becomes evil and pernicious in the face of the new thing which now comes. Hence Marcion speaks no longer—as Paul spoke —merely of the new creation of God, but of a "new God" (*Deus novus*).

For Marcion the God of the Old Testament and of the creation of this world became an evil God. For Paul the history of the Old Testament belonged to the past, but it was not obliterated. He took it up as promise into his gospel. In the epistle to the Hebrews the old covenant is seen as foreshadowing the new. But for Marcion the division between the old and the new runs not only through man, not only through heaven and earth, but also through God himself. Thus the history of the new gives rise to a metaphysical dualism. The new, strange God of Christ succeeds the old Creator of the world and destroys him. Redemption destroys creation, the gospel destroys the law, and faith becomes the enemy of the whole of known reality. But in this antithesis the new cannot bring salvation. It means annihilation. As there is nothing of which it can be predicated, it becomes basically unacceptable. But in fact, as we have said, the new is never wholly new. It is always preceded by a dream, a promise, an anticipation; otherwise we could not grasp and accept it, and it could not be effective in history.

When the universal church excluded Marcion as a heretic, it lost for itself the category of the new. As is always the case with the exclusion of heresies, the church became more united, but also poorer. Since then God's revelation has no longer been proclaimed in terms of the new and of freedom for the future, but with the authority of what is old and always true. No longer is the *incipit vita nova* announced, but a *restitutio in integrum,* not the beginning of a new life but the restitution of the old in its integrity. The lost paradise, of which even the sinner still has a fragmentary memory, is won back through Christ and the church. The original relation between creation and Creator is restored in grace. The old naturalistic notion of *die Wiederkehr des Gleichen,* the return of what was, dominates Christian hope. We recall the words of Augustine: "That which is now called the Christian religion was also there among the men of former times. Indeed from the very beginning of the human race until Christ appeared in the flesh it has never been absent. From then on the true religion which already existed began to be called the Christian religion" (*Retrac-*

tiones I, 12). Thus it is no longer "the new" but "the old" which now becomes the warrant for the truth of Christianity.

With Marcion, the Pauline stress on the newness of the order brought by Christ was also lost for the church. It was only because she retained Marcion's "New Testament" in the canon that the church stored up for herself her own permanent revolution. Today we must bring about this revolution. We have no right to postpone it further and to live on the basis of this delay. One can indeed ask whether or not Christianity became unfaithful to its origin in neglecting the category of the new. In any case, one will have to go quite far back in order to discover the role of Christianity in the history of God's promises and to actualize it in the contemporary world.

V. Perspectives of the New in the World Today

It is surprising that the category of the new has for centuries scarcely been considered by philosophers and theologians, even though it should provide the chief concept for every philosophy of history and paraphrase the most valuable element in Christian hope. It is only today that we find in Ernst Bloch a magnificent philosophy of hope,[3] in which the new is made the central theme. Ernst Bloch is himself a modern *homo viator* who has travelled through different lands and philosophies. In World War I he emigrated as a pacifist to Switzerland. During the Hitler period he fled to Prague, to Zurich and then to the United States. After World War II he returned to East Germany. In 1961, he, as a Marxist, had to flee from a so-called Maxist country. Today he lives in Tübingen. Ever seeking justice and freedom, and constantly meeting with disappointments, he sets before us a secular hope which has been sustained through many sufferings. He is a Marxist with a Bible in his hand, who hoped for greater things than socialism was able to give. He is a messianic thinker for whom the philosophy of the younger Marx pointed out the practical way to the fulfillment of prophetic promises. From him Christians can gain courage for their own hope.

For Bloch all reality arises from a sea of possibilities. From this sea of possibilities emerges again and again a new piece of reality. The world is not a prefabricated house but an open process. Likewise man does not yet have his true being in himself. He does not yet know what he properly is. Hence men seek in common the homeland of true humanity. The place where the future of men and of the world is decided is the present. This present is the front-line of the future. It is only if we know what we hope for and desire that we can gain the future at the front-line of the present. Otherwise we miss it and destroy it. The future can bring nothing and everything, heaven and hell, life and death. Hence the future is full of salvation and also full of danger. How is the open world-process decided? Through the militant courage of present hope. Bloch looks for men of hope, a "company of anti-nothing" who on the basis of their hope refuse to abandon the world to evil, inhumanity and the powers of destruction, since they remain true to the utopian dream of complete salvation. That for him is the dawn of the resurrection at the end of the world—death being swallowed up by victory. But for Bloch such a gleam of hope is maintained in its dawn only through human decision. This hope for salvation must be joined to what is now objectively possible in the world if it is to become practical and to reduce through attack the areas of the negative and of evil death.

In the new, which emerges at the present front-line of the

future and becomes possible, the ultimately new (*novum ulti-mum*) is always involved. Hence in what is temporally new we must recognize what is eschatologically new, seeing in the fragment the coming whole and in the potsherd the beauty of the perfect thing. If we aim beyond the present at this ultimate future, we hit the mark today. This power of transcending in hope gives us the freedom to do what is right now and will help further in the future. With Ernst Bloch the eschatological hope joins the possibilities of historical activity in the sphere of what is not yet (*des Noch-Nicht-Seins*).

That is a magnificent conception. Nevertheless, the question remains open: What does this hope accomplish in the sphere of that which is no longer (*des Nicht-Mehr Seins*)? In Bloch's thought the hope for the new thing of the future is linked with what men can do. But don't we need also a hope which is connected with what we must endure in sacrifice, in suffering and in dying? We need hope when we are young. But don't we need hope also when we are old and powerless, when we can no longer help ourselves, and when finally death robs us of all hope? Don't we need hope also for those who are gone, for the dead, in order to abide in love? Here the militant optimism of *Das Prinzip Hoffnung* is silent. There is for Bloch a hell on earth—and even worse, one in which there is no Easter. There is a dying in which the principle of hope can effect nothing. "Ever since Auschwitz, to fear death means to fear something worse than death"—was the objection of his friend T. W. Adorno, who did not wish *Das Prinzip Hoffnung* to become illusionary vis-à-vis that nihilism which we can have right here on earth.

Where, then, does Bloch's positive hope preserve the negative element? Where is the cross found in this hope? Christian theology must go further; it discerns in the crucified Christ the deepest abyss of godforsakenness and hopelessness on earth, but it also believes in Easter. Out of chaos, darkness and flood God created the world. In the context of nothing he revealed his creative power. Out of the humiliated, poor and abandoned Jesus who was crucified in disgrace, God makes his Messiah of the future, of freedom and of life. He justifies those who have been godless. He makes evil human beings his friends. He will raise the dead. If Christians, because of this God, hope for the future, they hope for a *Novum ex nihilo* and hence embrace in their hope in God, the creator of the future, all that is destroyed and hopeless. Out of that-which-is-not-yet something new can always come into being. That is fully possible. But can something new also come to be out of that which is nothing? This is the hope of Christians, since they not only join the "company of anti-nothing" and fight for the renewal of the world, but they enter as well into fellowship with the sinners, the poor, the abandoned and the dying. If God creates what is new out of nothing, then the poor, the abandoned, and the dying are closer to him than the efficient and militant heroes who help mankind. The rich and the powerful must take up the cause of the poor and the powerless, in order to effect for them a new future. But they must realize that in their turn the poor and repudiated represent them, since it is they who are visibly handed over to the might of death, in terms of which God will show his power.[4] They help others to recognize hope in God. If we bring both points together, we can now describe the new front-line of Christianity in the present.

The kingdom of God comes to those who are in misery and are heavily burdened. By coming to the poor and the wretched and calling to himself the suffering and those who are heavily burdened, Jesus, the Messiah of the new, shows that through poverty, hunger and exploitation man is held in a situation that is unworthy of him, and that it belongs to the new humanity to be satisfied, happy and independent. The kingdom which he proclaims is not only the beatitude of souls, but just as much *shalom*, peace and freedom on earth. "The body . . . is for the Lord, and the Lord for the body," says Paul (1 Cor. 6:13). But if the Lord belongs to the body, then Christians are called upon to demonstrate through their deeds his lordship over the starving, oppressed and exploited bodies of the poor. That is not merely Christian charity, but the proof of hope in the redemption of the body and the resurrection of the flesh. The church with its faith in the other world has often confined itself to "god and the soul." Hence hope for the redemption of the body shifted away from the church to the political revolutions. As Ernst Bloch says, consciously using biblical language, "The social utopia sketched in advance the conditions in which those who labor and are heavily burdened disappear." Through the critical analysis of industrial society's inner failures this social hope can be joined with present possibilities and become practical. If Christians would recognize here the spirit drawn from their spirit, they would take such a share in politics as would improve relations within human societies and between peoples. If they grasped that it is there that their proper hope for God's new creation takes on flesh, they would cooperate wholeheartedly, and not with their left hand only.

God's justice comes to the oppressed and injured. By coming to sinners and tax-collectors and those who hunger after justice, Jesus, the Messiah of the New, shows that man is held in an unworthy situation not only through poverty but also through lack of rights. Men hunger after recognition and inde-

pendence as well as bread. The kingdom which Jesus proclaims brings justice on earth. Hence Jesus celebrates with
those deprived of their rights the joyful eschatological meal of
the righteous and rejects the Pharisees, who have justified
themselves. Paul proclaims the gospel of God's justice for all
the godless, Jews and Gentiles alike. This gracious righteousness justifies sinners, makes God's enemies into God's friends.
It raises up the lowly. But if God, through the justification of
the godless, wishes to assume his rights upon earth, then Christians are called upon to demonstrate his rights by comforting
the humiliated and interceding for the injured. To a great extent the revolutionary movements in Africa and Asia today
are, as is well known, declarations of independence. What is at
stake is the fundamental right to be free and to shape one's
own life so as to be able to live it in a human fashion. They are
revolutions of self-confidence and self-respect, struggles
for identity in a repressive society. How much of the overseas
aid with which these countries are supplied by the rich industrial nations contradicts this self-respect and makes these men
dependent? On the other hand, social revolutions and programs for prosperity repeatedly mean the abandonment of
justice, freedom and independence, as can be frequently seen
in socialism. The two things belong together: there is no
human happiness unless dependence and subjection end; there
is no human dignity unless destitution comes to an end. In the
traditional doctrines concerning natural rights, we know how
those who lacked human rights were held to have rights before
God, even if generally these rights were justified in a static and
retrospective way. In these doctrines there always remained
alive an intention directed towards that future in which man
walks erect: "Now when these things begin to take place, look

up and raise your heads, because your redemption is near"
(Luke 22:28). "Natural law constructed relations in which
the oppressed and the injured disappear," says Ernst Bloch.
From the Christian standpoint he is correct; for, as Paul says,
through justification the sinner gets the right to lift up his head
before God and inherit the coming kingdom, servants become
free sons. For the sake of this divine righteousness which
comes to them, Christians will, as far as possible, seek to secure
the rights and self-esteem of the dispossessed.

God himself comes to man. Finally, it cannot be overlooked
that Jesus, the Messiah of the New, forgives sins, as only God
can forgive them, frees the guilty from the burden of their past
and thus gives to the dying, hope in the resurrection of the
dead. It is not only through outward poverty and humiliation
that man becomes inhuman, but also through the forces within
himself—the sin in his life and the power of death. The kingdom, which Jesus preaches through his very existence on earth,
is at bottom resurrection and eternal life. The Fourth Gospel
proclaimed that in the clearest way. It would be an error if
Christians today were to spend themselves only in social and
political initiatives. If there were no hope in the face of guilt
which could not be undone through new good intentions, if
there were no hope in the face of mankind's last enemy, death,
then all the social and political activity would be only an improvement of living conditions in the prison of the world, and
not a breaking out of the prison. Proclaimed as the resurrection and the life, Christ won the hearts of men. At death all the
hopes of mankind fail. It is only in the resurrection that they
gain their true power which overcomes the world. For that is
the most precious content of hope. By remembering and making present the resurrection of the crucified Christ this hope

gains its enduring basis. Through faith, power is taken from
death. Through the forgiveness of sins the bonds of guilt are
broken. Thus godless men come into full fellowship with God. It
is not in social utopias and a revolutionary natural law that
we find this reality. We find it in the church. For the church
exists where the word of reconciliation is brought to the un-
reconciled life. The church exists where, through the sacraments, the "power of the resurrection" is brought to a life
which is emptied by death. Here we find hopes for an absolute
and wholly new future, in which the contradictions that go
beyond merely social and political contradictions are to cease,
in which our understanding of the world in all its previous
relations also changes. Hence the Christian hope for the kingdom of the resurrection and of life does not coincide with a
social utopia or with a natural law. At the same time it is
through this hope that the social vision of love and the power
to think out man's legal rights can always be stimulated afresh.
The new thing which the church and the church alone stands
for is this: "Behold, the dwelling of God is with men. He will
dwell with them, and they shall be his people." The one who at
the beginning said, "Let it be," and who says at the end, "I
make all things new," will be in the midst of men (Rev.
21:3f).

What must a church look like which is given over to this
future of God? She would have to sever every alliance with the
existing powers (which as a matter of fact are passing away)
and unite herself utterly with the new situation of the coming
God. She would then become a "powerless teaching authority of
the conscience" with a view to the true future, the "ship of
the church free from superstition and on her way" (Ernst
Bloch). She would still be "religious" only in the sense that she

portrays—however inadequately—her link with the past as a complete dream for the future. Finally she would become ecumenical and catholic, in representing solidarity and fraternity in a world which is concerned only with the management of things. It is for such a church that the disillusioned atheists are waiting today. The way to this renewal of the church can be found if Christian faith extends itself to include hope in God, if our thinking moves from the "other world" to the future, from the church to the kingdom, from religion to the really new life and from the repetition of tradition to the realization of the promise held in remembrance. This will be a church of beggars and rebels, of men who look up and raise their heads because redemption is near. It will only be of this church, which stands solely for Jesus' Testament of God's new creation, that one will be able to say: She is the sacrament of hope for the earth. For in the potsherds of the present church one will be able to recognize the coming kingdom.

The language of the new order which is to come dare not be a speaking in tongues. We can infer from the prophets, and from the apostles as well, that it is expressed in at least three forms:

(1) A negation of what is experienced as negative. Even if the order which is to come can not be experienced as yet, we can already say what will no longer be: "Death shall be no more, neither shall there be mourning nor crying nor pain any more, for the former things have passed away" (Rev. 21:4). The coming truth is not as yet self-evident, but it is already at work in history as the indicator of the false (Bloch, Adorno). Even if we do not as yet know what true humanity is, we do already know very well what real inhumanity is.

(2) There are in history, under this presupposition of the

negation of the negative, always ready analogies in the form of anticipations and adumbrations of the new things to come. Freedom, justice, and beauty, in this world which will pass away, can be understood, despite their transiency, as a preview and foretaste of future fulfillment.

(3) Between the expectation on the basis of experience and promise, on the one hand, and the coming fulfillment, on the other hand, we must always take note of the element of the surprising and the sudden. Promises and expectations do not prejudice the future if they are directed towards a future that is created out of the freedom of God. They must be open and must unlock the human spirit for the unexpected, the sudden and the surprising in God's history. They must be so flexible that they can be revised by new situations. In this respect the Christian faith cannot be understood as a prejudgment of the future of God. It contains "unfaith" in the sense that it must say to itself: "I can hardly believe it." It thus retains an openness for the element of surprise in the fulfillment of its hope. This openness for the freedom of God will guard it against far-fetched dogmatic claims about the future.

NOTES

[1] *The Holy Bible,* Revised Standard Version (New York, Nelson, 1946, 1952). The Scripture quotations in this chapter are from this version, copyrighted 1946 and 1952 by the Division of Christian Education of the National Council of Churches.

[2] G. von Rad, *Theologie des Alten Testamentes,* II, 262.

[3] *Das Prinzip Hoffnung,* 1959.

[4] *My People Is the Enemy* (New York: Anchor, 1966).

SUGGESTED READING

Bloch, Ernst. *Das Prinzip Hoffnung* (Frankfort: Suhrkamp Verlag, 1959).

Harnack, Adolf von. *Marcion und das Evangelium vom fremden Gott.*

Käsemann, Ernst. *Exegetische Versuche und Besinnungen* I (Goettingen: Vandenhoeck and Ruprecht, 1960).

———*Essays on New Testament Themes,* trans. W. J. Montague, *Studies in Biblical Theology* (London: SCM, 1964).

Moltmann, Jürgen. *Theology of Hope* (New York: Harper and Row, 1967).

Von Rad, Gerhard. *Old Testament Theology,* I and II, trans. D. M. G. Stalker, (New York: Harper and Row, 1962, 1965.)

LANGDON GILKEY

The Contribution of
Culture to the Reign of God

Dr. Langdon B. Gilkey, Professor of Theology at the Divinity School of the University of Chicago, is one of Protestant theology's most distinguished and articulate representatives. The clarity, openness, and rigor of his thought has also made him a sought-after contributor to the ecumenical dialogue; witness his address on "Modern Myth-Making and the Possibilities of Twentieth-Century Theology," before the Congress on the Theology of Renewal of the Church, conducted in Toronto in 1967 under the auspices of the Catholic Bishops' Conference of Canada. His essay, "The Contribution of Human Culture to the Reign of God," contained herein adds a significant chapter to a growing body of his reflections on secularity and Christian hope.

A background of teaching at Union Theological Seminary, New York, Vassar College, and Vanderbilt University Divinity School has been complemented and fortified by research at Cambridge University as a Fulbright scholar and at Munich and Rome as a Guggenheim scholar.

The fruits of his activities are available in books and in articles: *Shantung Compound* (New York: Harper and Row, 1966); *How The Church Can Minister to the World Without Losing Itself*

34

(New York: Harper and Row, 1964); *Maker of Heaven and Earth* (New York: Doubleday, 1959); "Social and Intellectual Sources of Contemporary Protestant Theology in America," *Daedalus* (Winter 1967); "Providence in Contemporary Theology," *Journal of Religion,* 43 (July 1963); and "Cosmology, Ontology, and the Travail of Biblical Language," *Journal of Religion,* 41 (July 1961).

THE SCOPE of our topic, the contribution of culture to the reign of God, is immense: it includes, like the creation itself, all of heaven and earth, and then considers as well the work of God therein. From our human side, so to speak, it asks about the relation of culture, of the "secular," as we now call it, to the widest purposes and *telos* of history—hardly a confining topic. From the side of doctrines, it concerns questions of the interrelation of the fundamental notions of creation, providence, sin, and eschatology. We have before us, then, a very wide realm of discourse called culture and theology; I suggest that we try to map it out in terms of the question which I take to be the point of my title, namely, How, exactly, is the secular, the whole historical enterprise of culture, related to eschatology, to the final and complete manifestation of the rule of God? This question is a gnawing one, and the reason, let us note, is that the two most influential—i.e., the "in"—theologies of the present seem dramatically to divide on just this issue.

The secularizers, radical or otherwise, say that it is in and through the secular, in the structures and particularly the developments, of present culture and society, that God's reign comes to us. God is to be found, not in church, not in pulpit, not in chalice—nor in the eschatology of Mark or the Revelation of John—but in the streets, in the tensions, the struggles, and the achievements of the secular order. This is, let us note, a theology centered on the doctrine of providence: not in the Word but in the world is God achieving his ends. On the other hand, the liveliest theologians of the contemporary continent —for example, the distinguished German theologians Jürgen Moltmann and Johannes B. Metz—speak a quite different theological language: God is not now in the world, nor was he there at the beginning; he *will* be in the Eschaton. Now the world is Godless, a chaos or void as at the creation; the divine presence now is only in the church through the Word, and there it is the negation of the world in the cross, and at best a prolepsis for the future. Thus the gospel points us *out* of the present in both culture and church *into* the future when God comes. There is here, apparently, a radical denial of the importance of the doctrines of God's present activity through creation, and so of the relevance of culture, secular or otherwise, to theology and our understanding of God. It is on this debate that we shall base our remarks. And let me express first a word of appreciation to this new eschatological theology; its emphases on possibility, on the future, and on the objectivity of history are immensely important, and I have learned much from it.

In September 1967 Harvey Cox said in an address in Rochester: "This has been a bad summer for the secularizers. The major movements of the recent past, namely the revolutionary Black Power movement and the hippies, have (a) been violently anti-secular or anti-culture, an attack from different flanks on the secular culture of our age, and (b) have had a religious, or at least an eschatological, character to them. Thus the secular seems to be saying to us, 'We are losing our faith in the secular and are turning to religion, to the themes of spiritual withdrawal and of eschatological destruction to find our identity and meaning.' " We might comment that the latent ambiguities of secular life, the deep threats of meaninglessness and of demonic destruction concealed in the secular myths of scientific and moral progress, are revealing themselves in these potent secular repudiations of the role of culture in the reign of God. Cox admitted ruefully, but confidently, that a return to the drawing board might be a good idea. Our question then is, Should we, having found the work of providence in and through the secular order so ambiguous, shift our theological attention from providence to eschatology, cease to look for God in present culture and its history and look *only* to the eschatological future, to the coming God who *is* only insofar as he *will be,* whose sole presence now is that of a Word of promise for the end of things? Does the present secular order provide neither concepts nor materials for Christian hope, has it no contribution to make to the coming of the kingdom? And is theology therefore to fashion itself in no way on the world and God's providential work therein but only, on the one hand, on the revealed biblical Word of eschatological promise and, on the other, on the eschatological future out of which God is coming towards us?

In a strange and ironic sense, of which more in a while, many of the themes of the new eschatological theology are familiar—in fact, almost too familiar—to Americans. There is the same emphasis on change and becoming and on the future; on the reality of possibility, the inescapability of novelty, the significance of the new, as opposed to sacred tradition, a predetermined history, a static being, a changeless order, and an eternal present. This is an emphasis which in the past dominated the thought of American philosophers William James and John Dewey, and A. N. Whitehead's in particular; and at present it finds expression in the thought of Charles Hartshorne. There is furthermore the claim, made long ago by the Social Gospel, that not only is theology historical, as opposed to cosmological, but it must be political in its essential thrust and character. Valid Christianity represents a theology for revolutionary change of the social order, as Walter Rauschenbusch often said. Nothing has been so characteristic of American theological thought as these two notions, and for nothing else—except their lack of German learning—have Yankee theologians been so taken to task by their German colleagues as for these two emphases on the luminosity of the new and on the significance of politics and sociology for theology. Perhaps we might say, if somewhat facetiously, that the "bugs" in such a temporalist and political understanding of Christianity appeared to American theologians at about the time that European sirens were powerfully seeking to beguile them; and thus this typically American temporalist framework was overlaid with existentialist, inward, and transcendent emphases which we have learned to absorb from Europe just when our continental friends, who beguiled us in the first place, arrived to tell us of political theologians and the wonder of the new!

There is, however, a characteristic difference between the older American version of a theology built ontologically on a temporal becoming into the future, and morally on a social transformation, and its recent German nephew. In the American version, it was an understanding of the providential workings of God in the course of history which grounded both of these aspects, whereas in the continental version it is an eschatological understanding of God's activity and of his relation to us that is the fundamental motif. Not then, not now, but in the coming time is God at work, and what he will do in his future is to create the new out of the nothing of the past and the present. And it is this theological difference, this emphasis on God's work in the course of history, that gave the American version its positive relevance to culture as the basis for the ultimate achievement of the kingdom of God, and in turn has caused the negative relation of the modern German version to present culture as the antithesis of God's rule, as the *nothing* that precedes the divine creative action. In this chapter I shall support the liberal view.

Historical developments in both past and present culture *are* relevant to the rule of God, if that is to be meaningfully conceived in theology, and thus there can be no intelligible eschatology without a strong conception of the workings in the present of the divine providence. Our argument can be put in two criticisms of current eschatological theology as a useful mode of contemporary theologizing: (1) it assumes too much about the Word and the Eschaton to be intelligible to modern men, and thus raises all the problems of atheism it seeks to avoid; (2) it assumes too little about God's present action in creation and providence to make its own assumptions internally consistent. There can be no meaningful speech about God in the future, no eschatological theology of the reign of God, unless we assume his presence in the present cultural situation in which and out of which we speak about that reign; and there can be no meaningful or creative *action* for that future, unless we assume the creative activity of God within the past and within the present. Eschatology depends, therefore, on a positive relation of faith to present culture, and thus on an understanding of the activity of God in the present *saeculum*. Culture *does* contribute, through the creative work of God's providence and the more dubious work of human creativity, to the ultimate reign of God.

We can perhaps best defend the validity of this thesis by showing how culture, and therefore also providence, contributes to the possibility—that is, the meaningfulness—of an eschatological theology. To be itself intelligible, an eschatological theology must, we say, assume the positive role of culture in ecclesiastical and theological life, and thus the past and present work of God therein—and this is what we shall try to show. An eschatological theology without this assumption is in danger of contradicting itself. It maintains that God is only future Lord, not present providential Lord, and that therefore culture is now quite Godless and Godforsaken, symbolized theologically only by the negations of the cross, of death, and of nothingness, the nothing out of which divine creativity will mold the future. *Now* God is present only proleptically, as promise for the future, and only "religiously," in incarnation, church, word, sacrament, and spirit—he is not present creatively in secular historical culture. Thus is theology in methodological form biblical, in substantial content eschatological, and in ethical drive revolutionary. On the other hand, this form of theology is dependent throughout, both formally and materially, on historical and therefore cultural developments, and thus on the very providential presence and work of God which it denies. To prove this latter point, and so the contradiction, let us look first at the *formal* dependence of this type of theology on culture and so on providence—that is, its dependence on cultural history for ideas, categories, and the intelligibility of theological speech.

First of all, we must clarify some of the linguistic confusions present in modern eschatological theology. Often they speak as if God were *only* future, *only* coming, with the effect of making eschatology not only the last chapter of systematic theology but the sole remaining one. It is as if in the twentieth century we had tried to understand Christianity through all the other doctrines—revelation, creation, providence, anthropology, the incarnation, and the church—had found each one wanting, and were now settling in on the final one. For an example, Professor Moltmann has said, in an important paper, "God is *not* the ground of this world, and *not* the ground of existence, but the God of the coming kingdom";[1] and, "God is not 'beyond us' or 'in us' but ahead of us in the horizons of the future open to us in his promises."[2] And thus the deity of God is, and is to be spoken of, only in connection with his coming kingdom.[3] God seems here to be *only* future, and the language of theology thus *only* eschatological language: in the past there was, in the present there is, no deity; hence, instead of a "death of God," there will be in the future, so to speak, a "birth of God." But clearly this is not, and cannot be, what is meant at all. For as both Professor Moltmann and Father Metz make clear, and as one of the quotations above implies, we know of this future God only through the incarnation and the Word of God. The content of these theological notions may be eschatological, promises for the future; but their actuality as *known*, as something revealed by God to us, establishes that God *was present* at some point, at least in the incarnation, in order to reveal his Word, and that he *is present* now—enough, at least, to mediate this word of promise to us in the Spirit.

So the future eschatological categories are joined at least by theological categories referent to God's past and present action

—namely, the Word, the incarnation, and the Spirit. Presumably, moreover, if these events and activities are to be intelligible, creation must be added to them if theology is to escape
poor Marcion's difficulties, which, I gather, neither Father
Metz nor Pastor Moltmann wishes to encounter. Thus what
they are saying, perhaps not too clearly, is *not* that there was
no creator nor that there is no providential Lord at all—no
incarnation, word, church, or present grace—that God neither
was nor is, but only will be. Rather their point is, or must be,
that eschatology is the *clue* to the difficult meanings for our
age of these other doctrines, the key that unlocks their intelligibility in our situation, and that by interpreting these doctrines eschatologically in the present situation we will avoid the
dangers of meaninglessness in theology. Thus in another more
guarded, and so much more illuminating, passage, Moltmann
says: "God is the future of *every* present; he is past and
present, but always as future, as the principle *and promise of its
becoming, not as the substance of its being*"[4]—a very fine
expression of one of the great ideas in much contemporary
process philosophy. But at the moment our point is that the
actuality of God and the effectiveness of his work in the past
and present as well as in the future is here assumed, so that
despite frequent apparent denials, the notions of creation,
providence, revelation, incarnation, and so on, are present in
some form at least implicitly. Eschatology is the *clue* to the
intelligibility and meaning for our age of these doctrines; it
does not replace them.

The question I wish to raise here, however, is whether the
intelligibility of any doctrine for our secular age can really be
achieved, in either Europe or America, by merely interpreting
it in terms of another doctrine—as if one could redeem a ten-

spot in a dubious currency by cashing it on two fivers of the same currency. The assumption of an eschatological theology of the Word is that the previous theology, which, it maintains, encouraged atheism, was a theism based on the doctrines of creation, providence, or an accomplished incarnation—and that *this* is what causes difficulties to modern man. Correspondingly, if we interpret the whole biblical gospel through the key of biblical eschatology, these problems at least will be solved and Christian faith will begin to make sense in our time.

To me this is to miss the real point of the present problem of theology. The problem is that religious or mythical language of *all* sorts, of which biblical language is one variety, is difficult if not unintelligible to our age. By mythical or religious language, I mean not just an older mythical cosmology, but all those types of discourse which refer to the transcendent, which therefore contain transempirical language referring to what is transcendent to, and yet active in, nature and history. And my point is that whether the God who transcends nature and history is thought of as having been in the past, of being now in the present, or as coming only in the future, as active in nature *or* active in history, at the beginning or at the end, *none* of this fits into the world of reality and of intelligibility in which the modern man lives, and so all of these symbols are, to all intents and purposes, equally "queer" to modern men. The magician Bultmann pulled a sleight of hand and bewitched European theology into believing that the only *mythical* forms of language offensive to the modern consciousness were those primitive forms referent to the cosmos. Thus, the tradition of biblical theology has held that a language descriptive of God's acts in history, in the Exodus, in Christ, and at the end of time, was

not caught in the same difficult, if not hopeless, situation as
was cosmic myth. But modern man assumes a nexus of finite
relations among historical events as much as he does among
natural ones. He assumes, therefore, that there are in that
nexus no relevant factors that are not material, psychological,
or social in character; thus he takes it for granted that no
transcendent or divine factor really effects anything in the
course of history. This is the way he writes history and probably the only way he can understand what happened in it. As a
consequence kerygmatic and eschatological language is as much
myth to him as is the cosmogonic language of earlier religious
traditions.

Now if this be true, and I think it is, it means that the
meaning of the entire system of biblical language is the fundamental problem of theological intelligibility and poses the
original and major theological problem of a secular age. This
problem cannot be solved by the interpretation of other doctrines within that system of language in terms of one of the
doctrines of that system, even the last one. It can be settled
only by showing the contemporary relevance of religious language as a genre or as a whole to the current joys, crises, and
hopes of man as he experiences himself in the present. And
that in turn requires, I believe, a prolegomenon to theology
which shows the religious dimensions, the presence and the
absence of deity, in present secular experience—in other
words, that demonstrates the religious dimensions of culture
and, doctrinally speaking, the workings of God's providence,
of his judgment and grace, in our ordinary lives. The intelligibility of biblical language to a secular age, and so the intelligibility of the mythical language of eschatology, depends on the
relations of this whole form of language to present cultural
experiences of meaning, of despair, of conflict, and of hope—

on the present reality of the divine and the demonic in our experience. Eschatology, as a mode of language, is formally dependent on culture and the religious analysis of culture, if it is to be intelligible to us.

Secondly, present-day eschatological theology is formally dependent on the development of culture because its own formative notions have come to it, not right out of the Bible, but in fact from the slow development of ideas in secular Western society. The modern lively forms of eschatological theology—at least in Europe—are, thank heaven, not like older forms that cautioned us to allow a changeless God to wind it all up in his own good time, and therefore warned us not to be concerned about historical developments, justice, peace, and so on. On the contrary, modern eschatology consciously identifies its concept of God with temporal movement: he will be, he is the future, he is essentially possibility, his deity will be accomplished, and so on. Albeit in biblical language, this is a close approximation to the developing deities of post-Hegelian and evolutionistic philosophies, and the important heritage of process, developmental and historical views of reality—from Hegel through Marx, Bergson, Alexander, Dewey, Whitehead, to Heidegger and Bloch—shines through every fundamental doctrinal statement of this theology. Here is an important cultural lineage for eschatological theology. Insofar as this quite secular lineage—whatever its ultimately biblical roots—is valid and contributes to, rather than destroys, theology—as this school so much in its debt must admit—the contribution of culture to the understanding of eschatology must likewise be admitted. And some view or other of the present workings of providence in and through even the philosophical notions of this Godless world must be affirmed.

The other new element in the new eschatology is its clear

concern for social justice: for the poor, the oppressed, the victims of war, and so on. This concern is not, as in the older eschatological theologies, merely for their immortal souls; rather the goal is that the situation of suffering man in this world be improved, and this, so they imply, is the primary thrust of an eschatological calling and their primary duty as Christians. Now this emphasis on human well-being, even material well-being, in this historical life, is also relatively new as a mode of interpreting Scripture, especially the eschatological elements of Scripture. It first occurs strongly among the Franciscans and the Brethren of the Common Life, reappears even more vigorously in the left wing of the Reformation, in many of the groups in the English Civil War, among the Quakers and later the Methodists; and finally finds its strongest and most self-conscious forms in the Social Gospel movement in America and in subsequent forms of Protestant liberalism. Nevertheless, all we churchmen must admit that despite this distinguished lineage of Christian social and political theologies, the main forces responsible for the present identification of God's will with social betterment, of eschatology with justice, equality, freedom, brotherhood, and an end to want, have been secular or cultural forces. The anti-clerical Enlightenment democrats and humanitarians, the socialistic idealists of the nineteenth century, the secular liberals of the Anglo-Saxon democratic traditions, the communist movement in all its forms, have so identified moral responsibility with responsibility for the material, social, and political well-being of my neighbor, whoever he is, that even our most conservative theological traditions and our historically most unhistorical and passive doctrines—for example, eschatology—now have the ring of active social reformism to them. Again secular culture has contributed to our understanding of eschatology, and above all—more significantly than probably have the churches —to whatever reality the social reign of God has amongst us. None of these modern theological interpretations of eschatology would have been possible, nor would what social justice there is have been achieved, without the work of providence in and through even the most anti-clerical and anti-biblical forces of our time.

In the most concrete sense, God will not be in the future as he promises to be if he has not already been, and if he has not been active in the life of secular culture, as well as in the promises given to the churches.

We have been arguing that eschatological theology is formally dependent on culture and so on the doctrines of the creativity of man and of God's work in creation and in providence—and by formal we have meant that both the intelligibility and the content of its language, its ruling ideas, depend upon the presence and the work of God in and through our cultural life. The implication is that if in truth the world be now quite Godforsaken, or a *nihil*, and especially if God be merely coming and not here in any sense, then the biblical language of eschatological hope is meaningless in that Godforsaken world, and the modern eschatologies of social betterment would never have come into existence, at least not as they actually did.

Now let us turn to the material and therefore more important side of the argument. Here we shall seek to show the contribution of past and present culture—not in this case to the conception of the reign of God, as that reign is interpreted by modern eschatologists, but to the realization of that reign as they understand it. The realization of God's reign as now interpreted is, as we have seen, intimately concerned with or relevant to the cultural problems of injustice, poverty, war, oppression, prejudice, and so on. God's future *answers* these crises that man alone in culture apparently cannot answer. The meaning of the divine future can and must in effect be understood as the negation of an oppressive and alienated present cultural reality, and thus the future of God has no meaning, as here interpreted, except in relation to these experiences of meaninglessness, of injustice, and of hopelessness in our worldly life. Eschatology here is not a call to a passive acceptance of the world, and so an indifference to its present cultural shape, as in the pietistic and evangelistic past, waiting, so to speak, outside the world in Christian patience for God to do it all. On the contrary, it is a call to battle creatively in the world against the world's ills, in the transcendent hope of the transformation of the human predicament. This is eschatology related to the category of revolution in history, to that of our active participation in the overturning of all the conditions that dehumanize man, and not to a withdrawal from history.

I have sketched the dependence of this conception of New Testament eschatology on developments among modern cultural ideas; now let us discuss the dependence of its realization on cultural and providential forces at work already in present history.

First of all, as we have noted, the meaning of the divine promise, so understood, is directly correlated with the cultural, social, or historical experience of meaninglessness, injustice, and hopelessness. For it is these "humiliations of man," we are told, which God's future promises to resolve. Culture thus does at least contribute to the reign so understood by producing the problems of which God's future reign is the answer. But these experiences of culture's tensions and distresses themselves depend in turn on the creative and providential presence of God in human existence. Let me explain. The capacity of man to search for, to find, and—corresponding with the capacity—to need meaning in life reflects a dim awareness of the ultimate horizon of meaning in which he exists. His need for living his life in a just and ordered relation to his neighbor, and in fact his most basic value questions themselves, reflect the presence of the divine will. Thus the category of hope, seeking as it does meaning and justification in the future, itself bespeaks man's existence *coram Deo,* in the presence of God, whether he is aware of this or not. Culture as a realm in which can arise such questions of meaning and meaninglessness, of justice and injustice, of hope and dread, is possible, I believe, because of the pervasive, hidden, mostly obscured but nevertheless essential, work of God in the life of man. We demand an ultimate meaning, a tolerable justice, and a secure hope in life because we have a dim awareness of being rooted in God, because we are already in relation to him. This essential but most unheeded—especially in a secular culture—relation to the sacred ground and horizon of our existence is the necessary condition of our cultural life. Thus the questions of social justice and of historical meaning, to which this eschatology is an answer, the *adventus Dei* as here pictured, have meaning for us and for our time only because the Lord is already at work in the world. Without that work of creation and providence we would not be men in search of a meaningful future at all.

This is not at all to say that the creative providence of God is ultimately the sole effective factor in the development and history of culture, as possibly Augustine and certainly the Reformers thought. Man is, for good or ill, the creator of culture.

But he can be creative in this way only because of the continual and irremovable presence of God as the ultimate source of his being, the ultimate context of his meanings, the ground of his valuings, and the locus of his hopes. Still he creates in freedom, and thus also in sin. This seems to me evident as well. Thus is culture, past and present, essentially ambiguous: sinful and oppressive as well as creative, meaningless as well as filled with meaning, hopeless as well as the generator of hopes. The theological categories of providence and of human freedom thus combine in the ambiguity of history, and as a consequence, truly drive towards eschatology, when the hidden reign of God will be at last manifest, when what is seen only in dim awareness, and so in obscurity, in ordinary experience, and in actuality and clarity only in Christ, in the cross and in promise—though there are some first fruits in culture and in the church!—is fully realized. Thus we agree that to subordinate eschatology to providence, or even to the completed gifts of grace in and through the incarnation, is to look out on the present world with smugness, and only upward and out of history with hope. Nevertheless, the entire historical and sociopolitical understanding of eschatology, however valid in its emphasis, falls into immediate self-contradiction if it seeks to exclude the fundamental presence of God in our cultural life, even in and through the sinful character of that life. The Word and the Spirit in the church are not the only modes of God's activity in the world. Were that so, the political and social life of our world would have none of its vital dissatisfactions, its urgent drives and its real purposive hopes, on each of which this theology depends.

Secondly, revolutionary transformation, which provides not only the theological but also, and especially, the ethical content of this interpretation of eschatology, is a cultural and historical concept. Social revolution refers to processes on the plane of history, processes generated by long and essential developments in culture, and any social transformation is both impossible and unintelligible without those developments. Any revolution in the future thus has its seeds in the present: on the one hand in the injustices, evils, and frustrations of the present, and on the other in the hidden, latent forces which will accomplish the overturn. The ideas governing any revolution have a long cultural development into the present, and the forces which these ideas direct and which carry them to embodiment are forces maturing in the present. Thus culture must contribute to the reign of God interpreted in socio-political terms, for revolution, no less than evolution, is a cultural word. Again the picture of the present world as quite Godforsaken, of the presence of God as only in the cross and the Word, and God as revealed only in the future, is vastly overdrawn if God's future comes into history, as apparently here it does, in intimate connection with the imminent, and so present, socio-political forces that accomplish revolution and, in intention at least, set right old social wrongs. If the advent of God's reign concerns revolutions against injustice and oppression, then a good revolution is itself a contribution of culture and its history to that eschatological reign—as Marx and all his philosophical followers knew well enough.

But let us now look at the other side of this same coin. Revolution is a cultural and historical word, we have said, and a revolution a very historical reality created by historical forces and dominated in its unfolding by those forces and by the men who direct or are directed by them. Sad as it may seem, one must insist that future revolutions will be just as

historical and cultural in this basic sense as were past ones, for
they will be conducted by men and not by angels. For while it
is true that the future is the arena of hope, and that progress,
even through revolution, is surely always possible, nevertheless
nothing in the future course of social history will transcend
these conditions of history itself, set for it by the ambiguities of
its chief actor, man. Sin, cruelty, injustice, as well as love,
compassion, and creativity, manifest themselves through all of
man's cultural activities, even his revolutionary programs, and
they will continue to do so. Nothing in social history will be
purely God's future, for men as yet unredeemed will help to
bring it about. Neither historical destiny nor our own sin ever
allows us in history to do completely or even partially what we
intend to do: the good we would we do not, and the evil that
we would not, that we practice—as our nation is surely
discovering sadly now, and as every past revolutionary group,
who were once the future, have discovered as their once open
future became the grim historical present. Let us remember
that our past was once another Christian age's future; and that
that past is now filled with and shaped by what were once
history's revolutions. Thus, if the revolutionary future is really
the arena of God's activity, that future and that activity will
become one day past, and become a part of the continuities of
culture, contributing both for good and ill into the future.
Thus does the eschatological future, if it be real and effective
in sacred history, become in time the work of past providence.
And, like all the works of providence combined sadly with
human freedom, it will become full of ambiguity and sin and
so generating through grace, hope and faith in the future to
come. Eschatology and providence, the future and the past,
divine promise and cultural history are dialectical or polar

concepts that imply and require each other if historical and temporal passage be real.

While, therefore, it is surely against the faith in God's providence and his promises to look with nothing but glum faces to the future, still it is even more against both the clear evidence and that faith to think that our political future, or even the future of the liberal or revolutionary cause we support now, is so connected with God's future as to make it qualitatively different from the past revolutions and causes of our other human brothers whose results form our present. If their future, realized now in our present, be a nothing, then why expect ours to be so different and to be clearly God's future?

This is the besetting spiritual sin of revolutionaries: to interpret their own future eschatologically rather than historically, to raise to the level of religious ultimacy the valid hopes and dreams of a better but not a perfect day. Eschatology too closely mixed with socio-political history is not a biblical notion; it is the besetting sin of secular political men throughout the ages and the explanation of their inordinate cruelty— whether it be Barabbas the Zealot, the Bourbon revolutionaries of eighteenth-century France, the Enlightenment revolutionaries of the American colonies, the early Communist revolutionaries of Russia and China, or the Nazi revolutionaries of recent Europe. Each thought he was bringing in a divine future qualitatively different from the sordid present. Just as the sin, and terrible it is, of groups with power is to make the present order that supports them into God's providential order and so to defend it with fanaticism and cruelty, so it is the sin of revolutionary classes to identify their own order in the future with God's future. Because it identifies darkness with the others' past and light with our own future, eschatology in poli-

tics is heady but dangerous brew. Such an identification of our
future with God is far more "secular" than "biblical," for to
me the biblical view of eschatology is primarily a guard, in fact
precisely a guard, against such political pride. And the reason
the biblical view is sounder is precisely that it refuses to identify God's action exclusively or even centrally with what will
be historically achieved in the future. We are, in other words,
wondering if it is either good politics or good theology to interpret Christian faith solely eschatologically, to locate the
alienation and sin of the world in separation from God in the
past and the presence of God solely in the future. And the
problem is that if we center on eschatology to the exclusion of
providence, judgment, and grace, the real biblical meaning for
eschatology is sacrificed and the concept becomes dangerously
secularized. Let us in our conclusion enlarge on why this is
so.

First of all, if God appears in each present moment solely as
the divine demand and the divine promise for the future, and
at most in Christ and the Word as prolepsis for the time to
come, then this surely becomes a gospel of law not of grace—
"the categorical imperative of the resurrected one," as Professor Moltmann says.[5] That is, the substance of the gospel is
here a call to us to act as co-workers for God's future, and
through our self-realization in self-renunciation we cure the
problem of our own self-estrangement and become thereby
aware of God's reality and deity. Thus, as is logically necessary
in the eschatological theology where promise is the only
present divine gift, what we do on earth is an autonomous
action, and not one based on grace, and is in fact creative of
our relation to God, and not its result. For there is now here
neither real judgment on our present nor real grace in our

present if God comes always only as future and as promise. But this Pelagian view of man and of history, in which men are able at the divine call to help usher in the kingdom, is surely against all the main threads of biblical theology, and contradictory to the evidence of history itself. If our freedom is to be creatively cooperative with God's purposes in history, it must be a freedom qualified and tempered by the *present* judgment of God on our past and present sins, and by the *present* operative grace of God in our contemporary situation: repentance, faith, and sanctification as well as hope are necessary if man is to be a co-worker with God. If eschatology is the sole clue to God's presence in history, then man's history will remain essentially unrelated to God's purposes, its conservative forces irredeemably oppressive and his revolutionary forces inescapably demonic, and this socio-political interpretation of God's future will have no historical ground on which to stand.

Finally, to interpret theology in exclusively eschatological categories is to lose the unique significance and function of biblical eschatology itself. That function, as this school agrees, is not to nullify the historical process, to wind it up arbitrarily at an end unrelated to its own course and therefore to our active work within it, as Protestant evangelical eschatology often affirmed. Rather, again for both of us, the function of the eschatological hope and promise is to make possible a creative Christian participation in the present struggles of history. To fill that function, we have argued, eschatology cannot so dominate our theology as to cancel out the work and presence of God in creation, in providence, and in special grace through the incarnation. For if it becomes the main key to *all* the activity of God, then, as we have seen, our political future and

God's future become inevitably identified—for that is the only meaning left for the now vacated symbol of God. In such a theology eschatology becomes a principle of criticism only on the past and the present (on the realized future of other people), and ceases to be a principle of criticism as well on the future we help to create; that is, it loses its most significant function. For that function is, I believe, to resolve the ambiguity of providence and of sin with both judgment and promise. The eschatological promise of the kingdom, of the final fulfillment in God, to be sure brings home to us that the world is as yet both incomplete and sinful, that it is by no means as yet what it ought to be, and that as Christians we are called to participate in its radical transformation. It challenges every tendency to sanctify the present, to regard the work of God as complete through incarnation, providence, and human creativity. But correspondingly, it challenges as well those who identify their political tomorrow with God's future. For that tomorrow, when it comes, will also be the work of both providence and human powers, and the more sure the men who now fashion it are that it is perfect, the less like God's future it will really be when it comes. Eschatology challenges both the defender of the status quo and the overturner of present structures, for both can distort the silent work of providence, both share our common sin, and both stand in the need of God's present grace. When it moves to the center of the stage, eschatology loses its legitimate and significant role as critic of future projects as well as of past achievements, and its great divine promises are in danger of becoming secular tyrannies.

Both theology and history are too simply understood in this form of theology. The ambiguity of our historical existence must be interpreted by the variegated symbols of creation and providence, sin, incarnation, judgment and grace, as well as by eschatology, if we are to understand and thus to transform the historical conditions that beset us. To understand history and God as dark in the past and light in our future is to create a new temporal dualism which obscures the vitality and ambiguity of history as much as did the older metaphysical dualism of matter and spirit. If God's future is to be meaningful, his work in the present as ruler, judge, and loving servant must also be actual; and if man's activity in the past has been only sinful, and so uncreative, there is no basis for assuming that his revolutionary action in the future will not again manifest only that same ambiguity and nothingness. We *can* believe in history despite this ever-present ambiguity, and can share in the reality of hope, but only because of the present activity of God as the ultimate unity of power and meaning that sustains and makes possible the human cultural enterprise, and we can face the future with confidence despite the darkness of destiny and sin because of the knowledge of the healing effects of God's judgment and his grace in his present Word. Without these evidences of the present reality of the divine power and love, there is little hope for the historical future, and so little ground for the identification of that future with God. Culture does contribute to the eschatological reign of God because both God's providence and his Word are at present at work in the world as the necessary conditions for creative hope and creative revolution.

NOTES

[1] These references are taken from Jürgen Moltmann's "Hope and History or Theology as Eschatology," 1967: a paper written for a symposium at Duke University, April 1968, p. 6.

[2] *Ibid.*, p. 5.
[3] *Ibid.*
[4] *Ibid.*, p. 8.
[5] *Ibid.*, p. 25.

SUGGESTED READING

Augustine, St. *De Civitate Dei.*
————*De Magistro.*
Calvin, John. *Institutes,* Bk. I.
Lonergan, Bernard F. *Insight* (New York: Philosophical Library, 1957).
Niebuhr, Reinhold. *Faith and History* (New York: Scribner's, 1949).
Rauschenbusch, Walter. *Theology for the Social Gospel* (Nashville: Abingdon Press) n.d.
————*Christianity and the Social Crisis* (Magnolia, Mass.: Peter Smith) n.d.
Ritschl, Albrecht. *Christian Doctrine of Justification and Reconciliation,* Vol. 3 (Clifton, New Jersey: Reference) n.d.
Tillich, Paul. *Systematic Theology,* 3 vols. (Chicago: University of Chicago Press, 1951, 1957, 1963).
————*Theology of Culture* (New York: Oxford University Press, 1959).
Whitehead, Alfred North. *Process and Reality* (New York: Macmillan, 1967).
————*Adventures of Ideas* (New York: Macmillan, 1933).

J. COERT RYLAARSDAM

The Old Testament and the New: Theocentricity, Continuity, Finality

The foundation of Christian hope was laid in the Old Testament. Therefore, an Old Testament scholar's view of The Future as the Presence of Shared Hope is essential to a treatment of the theme. In his essay, "The Old Testament and the New: Theocentricity, Continuity, and Finality," DR. J. COERT RYLAARSDAM, Professor of Old Testament Theology at the Divinity School of the University of Chicago, continues his exploration of the nature of the relationship between the Jewish and Christian faiths, both historically and in the present.

His recent professional activity includes representing the University of Chicago in the organization of the Jewish-Christian colloquium, "Perspectives on the Good Society," to which he contributed a lecture on "Common Ground and Difference"; membership on study groups of the World Council of Churches; co-editor of the *Journal of Religion,* and numerous lecture assignments.

In the field of Old Testament, Professor Rylaarsdam's published work includes *Revelation in Jewish Wisdom Literature* (Chicago: University of Chicago Press, 1946); "Proverbs, Ecclesiates and

Song of Songs," *Laymen's Bible Commentary* (Richmond: John Knox, 1964); "Common Ground and Difference," *Journal of Religion*, 43 (October 1963); "Exodus," *The Interpreter's Bible* (New York: Abingdon Press, 1952); and contributions to the *Interpreter's Dictionary of the Bible*, Peake's *Commentary on the Bible*, and *The Study of the Bible Today and Tomorrow.*

BEGINNING WITH St. Paul, Christian exegetes and theologians have explored the nature of the relationship between Judaism and Christianity from a number of primary, persistent perspectives: Christological, ethical, eschatological, and so on. Each one of these has its own peculiar merit in locating and analyzing both the bonds and the tensions that relate the two faiths. It is, however, becoming increasingly clear that when it is one's aim to accent differences and illumine the novelty of the New Testament, one is well-advised to choose the eschatological base as one's point of departure.

Historically Christian and Jew have differed most radically about the future; i.e., about hope. Their difference is about the way of fulfillment, as well as about the shape of it. And they also differ—just as irreconcilably—about the form or nature of the evidence or basis in the present to which their respective visions of the future can appeal. It should be pointed out at the outset that in respect to this latter difference, Christians have seldom agreed among themselves about their own position either—notably, as Protestants and Roman Catholics.

An apparent revolution is rocking the Christian theological world today. This revolution is rooted in the growing conviction that the classical formulations about hope in Christianity, whether about the nature of the present reality that serves as its warrant or the inferences therefrom that define its shape in the future, are no longer communicable in the current cultural scene.

I

In this chapter we wish to present the meaning of hope in the Jewish Bible. We want to do this, in part, by noting contrasts with its meaning in the Christian tradition. Further, because of the nature of the crisis in Christian theology, we want to concentrate on "the Presence of the Future . . ."—i.e., the nature of the present reality on which the hope rests. Though we are dealing with issues which are analogous to those of eschatology in Christian theology, we have, by design, avoided every form of that term in our title. Eschatology is a term coined by modern theologians to deal with the discontinuity between time and eternity; or, in the case of the New Testament, between the end of the old age and the incursion of the new. The Jewish Bible is not eschatological in either of those ways; nor is the Jewish faith. The term "continuity" in our title is meant to remind us of this. To broaden the applicability of the word eschatology by diluting its meaning, as some biblical theologians have done, among them von Rad, by simply making it a synonym for fulfillment of every sort, impairs its technical usefulness. At least with respect to our topic, its use would badly confuse the issues.

What is the nature of this crisis in Christian theology? It revolves around the function of the Christ-event in Christian faith. The New Testament and Christian tradition have historically assigned a double role to this event. It is both *Heilsgeschichtlich* and eschatological. The latter is in trouble.

Treated as an event in the story of salvation, the Christ-event continues the series that marks the great turnings in the long tradition of biblical faith: the birth of Isaac, the escape from Egypt, the conquest of the land, and so on. Like all of its predecessors, its import is this-worldly and incarnational. And, as in the case of each of them, faith finds in it a new insight into the human situation in the light of God's self-disclosure, to which all bear testimony. Thus, for example, in the Christ-event faith proclaims that with respect to its end in death human life in God's keeping is as secure as it is in its beginning, in Isaac. But despite the novelty, the scene remains the same. The event of revelation, like all its predecessors, constitutes the fulfillment of a promise; but it does not mark the end of the world. It is an event that reveals the action of God, but it does not displace it. The finality in the revelation belongs to the divine action, not to the event *per se*. The action continues, and its effect is cumulative. Thus the series of events is not necessarily finished. The role of nature and of man and his world in God's action as Creator and Redeemer remains what it was before. God will continue to visit the same old world he has always visited. The history of salvation goes on; in the theocentric action of God, Creation and Redemption remain coterminous.

Christianity and the New Testament, however, also treat the Christ-event as the eschatological event. It is the event that brings the story of salvation to an end, at least in the old scene. This is novel. The finality and freedom of God's action is equated with or displaced by the finality of the event. The old world has come to an end; it no longer serves the purposes of the divine action. A new, supernatural world has been superimposed on it. The event of salvation history that brought the

old world to an end is, simultaneously, the center of authority
and action in this new world. Theocentricity is summed up in
Christ; Creation is swallowed by Redemption. The old world
of time, space, and matter—including the old Adam—is shorn
of significance. The new age no longer needs the old. It may
depreciate and despise it; or it may tolerate and enjoy it. But,
in either case, its erstwhile meanings and functions have been
transcended. Both the Covenant of Noah and the Covenant of
Moses are said to have made way for, been summed up in, and
set aside by the New Covenant of grace. Not the continuity of
the work of God in nature, represented by circumcision, but
the discontinuity of Baptism, which separates the old world
from the new, is the sign of his action in Jesus Christ. Material
food and drink can no longer express the Kingdom; it has
become a spiritual reality. The Messianic Banquet is etherial-
ized; the New Adam moves in an eternity above flesh and time.
This eschatological treatment of the Christ-event is the nub of
the crisis in Christian theology today.

It should cause no surprise that the crisis is located where it
is. Modern man does not think eschatologically or dualisti-
cally. He is much more likely to think relativistically. In any
event, his orientation is monistic; his thoughts about God as
the living center of meaning and action assume that he medi-
ates himself in, through, and by means of the processes of time,
space, and matter. The impact of science and technology, the
criticism by Marxism and the social sciences, the evaporation
of mythological cosmology, and the displacement of Greek
philosophy and anthropology all point to this, whether as
cause, symptom, or result.

Though today's cultural climate has its own peculiar and
novel difficulties with the eschatological interpretation of the

Christ-event, the status of this interpretation has been a perennial source of crisis for Christian theology. Time and again the faithful have felt compelled to by-pass it, qualify it, or reformulate it; a history of Christian thought could use that "readjustment" with respect to the eschatological treatment of the Christ-event as the thread for its whole story.

In its apocalyptic setting in sectarian Judaism, Christianity was launched as a faith of eschatological fulfillment. The New Testament was a book about a new age; for nineteen centuries the church has been busy trying to naturalize it in the old. To this day, every new Christian sect or movement that springs from the impact of a New Testament unqualified by the main Christian tradition almost invariably begins as an otherworldly community, whether in an apocalyptic or existential sense; a colony of heaven in an alien world. The story of these groups, like the story of the entire Christian tradition, becomes the story of the progressive readjustment to the realities of the old world. The Adventists now constitute the elite cadres in the military medical corps of the old world's armies, the Nazarenes are building churches with stained-glass windows. Indeed, history shows that yesterday's heralds of a new age, who fled decay, wickedness, and time often end up as the most reliable and creative custodians of the values of the old order. The process of readjustment began in the New Testament itself: Luke-Acts re-emphasizes the continuity in history we call *Heilsgeschichte,* and even St. Paul, the most conspicuous apocalypticist, reinterprets the Parousia. It has never ended.

What is new about this old crisis is that its challenge takes a new form today. It is not so much a matter now of showing that this other-worldly eschatological faith has relevance for this old world, that it can do and say crucially important things in the world of time. That older way of putting it is set aside by a new one which asks not about the relevance of the faith for the world, but rather about the relevance of this old world of time, space, and matter for the action of the God implied by the faith that defines itself by the eschatological Christ-event. This reversal springs from the more radical secularity of modern man's existence. To the modern man, including the modern Christian, the traditional theological account of Jesus Christ seems sometimes to set up a barrier between the very real world of his human existence and the living God of the Bible. He wants to know whether the eschatological Word of God called Jesus Christ leaves real room for the continuity of theocentric, redemptive action in the order of Creation. Can he expect the revelation of God where he is most inclined to look for it? Does God still visit man in the old world?

Former theological adjustments in the eschatological interpretation of the Christ-event, for all their variety, always offered him help: how he might endure or make use of his natural and historical existence. He is not asking for that kind of help today; he wants to know whether he can protect some things he considers important from this announced finality. The continuity and faithfulness of the action of God in nature, set forth in the Covenant of Noah, makes sense to him. So, sometimes, does the utility and perfection of nature by grace represented by circumcision. He has been taught to read the Jewish Bible in the light of the New Testament and make it a Christian book. Today, as a modern man, he is tempted to reverse that process and look at the New Testament as an important but time-conditioned turning, to be understood in the light of a long tradition, another chapter in the story of salvation in which Creation and Redemption are held together.

He wants to interpret the New Testament in the light of the Old. In the past, Christian arrogance and Christian dogma combined to prevent this. The crisis in Christian theology may be too acute today, and the Hebrew Bible may be too relevant to it, to permit that dubious form of self-sufficiency to continue.

Now, surely, it is somewhat ironical that the greatest theological revival of our century should have pushed the crisis we have described to the breaking point. The neo-Reformation theologies of Barth and Bultmann, and, in a more qualified way, neo-Thomist theologies as well, emphasized anew the eschatological interpretation of the Christ-event; the Word of God in his sovereign freedom and action was liberated from its imprisonment in both nature and the works of men, notably philosophical structures and categories. But this was a Christocentric rather than a theocentric recovery and stressed the finality of an event with reference to its "otherness," *the* event in the order of Redemption which, for many today, stands as a barrier to the action of God in the order of Creation, where the crisis is located.

The theological revival was a repossession of the past in terms of the categories and structures of the past. Therefore we call it neo-orthodox. It surely tried manfully to assimilate the present cultural scene in its own terms; but it was both too Christocentric and too eschatological to do so.

The fact that this neo-orthodox phenomenon was somewhat more dramatic in its Protestant expression corresponds to the eschatological accent of the Reformers. The Reformation was an attempt to recover the New Testament in a manner less dependent upon tradition. Working with the eschatological discontinuity of the New Testament, notably in St. Paul, it rejected or qualified many of the "readjustments" embedded in fifteen centuries of the Catholic heritage. The ontological interpretation of the church as the body of Christ was scrutinized; its identification as the Kingdom of God was rejected; metaphysical interpretations of the faith became suspect; and the discontinuity between nature and grace was worked out cultically as well as theologically. The relation between empirical actualities in the present and the reality of future hope was relativized in the context of the work of the Holy Spirit and of faith. The doctrine and function of the sacraments were revised in a kerygmatic direction. The meaning of all material and temporal phenomena was undercut: places, times, authorities, relics and traditions. The *Incarnatus,* as a continuity in time, was largely set aside by the *Sursum Corda.* The finality of the Christ-event remained Christocentric, and its "once-for-all" in the old world was limited to a single chronological point. Eventually, of course, beginning with the absolutization of the written Bible, Protestantism was to write its own story of this-worldly "readjustment" in which an entirely new range of empirical temporalities, more often secular than sacral, came to serve as a present basis for future hope. That is the story of liberalism. But in this new story there was no reassertion of theocentricity either, though the eschatology of Christology was all but dropped.

The Protestant neo-orthodoxy of Barth and Bultmann spent a great deal of its energy repudiating liberalism and its new empirical basis for future hope, though the former, especially, enjoyed fighting the Reformation over again—just for the record, so to speak. Each in his own way reasserts the discontinuity between the old world and the new by employing the eschatological nature of the Christ-event. With respect to sac-

ramental theology and ecclesiology, Barth goes beyond the
Reformation. To be sure, in the later Barth *Heilsgeschichte* is
reintroduced and hailed as the "true history." But it is a
strange, non-empirical history, *sui generis*, affirmed in faith. In
the modern scene it offers no bridge of communication with
man's experienced world of nature and history. The theocentricity of the Word of God in Creation can not speak because
of the finality of its utterance in Redemption. The early Bonhoeffer, a zealous pupil of Barth, in the name of his eschatological dualism, scorned all human values and all humanitarian
judgments as unworthy of Christian attention. The results were
catastrophic for both Christianity and humanity.

For Bultmann the only function of the old world, epitomized in Israel and in the Hebrew Bible, is to demonstrate its
incapacity as the empirical carrier of hope. For Barth the old
world was subsumed under Christ the Word, even transformed
by him. Bultmann is not more eschatological, but he is more
apocalyptic, and Greek. For him the old world is overcome
and demolished in the decision of faith, which is the demythologized, apocalyptic End for everyman. The decision of faith is
lifted to the level of the Christ-event itself, it seems. Henceforth, man is "open to the future." It does not say "to the
world." The difference is not wholly unimportant.

Neo-orthodoxy's eschatological Christocentrism has pushed
the crisis in theology to the breaking-point. The crisis is about
Creation, about the function of the world of time, space, and
matter for God—of this world that is so important and meaningful to man. Is it possible to deal with this crisis from a
Christocentric standpoint historic in Christianity, by readjust-
ing the balance between the *heilsgeschichtliche* and eschatological dimensions of the Christ-event? Or are we challenged

to consider a more radical reorientation, from the Christocentric to the theocentric? Attempts at reorientation of that sort in the past have always proceeded from a Greek rather than from an Hebraic point of departure, by means of the universal categories of reason and philosophy. They have always miscarried, for in the end they were shown to have by-passed the heart of biblical faith, the reality of the action of God in the world of time and the reality of the people of God.

Despite the academic impressiveness of both Catholic and Protestant neo-orthodoxy, it seems that today the real growing edge of theology lies elsewhere. The entire focus of concern is shifting. Instead of seeking to describe the form of *Redemption*, which is the basis of hope, in terms of its present actuality this new theological urge asks about the present reality of the living God in *Creation*. Its focus is not only temporal instead of eschatological; it is also secular rather than sacred. Because it alludes to so many of these "grass roots" concerns—without, perhaps, being fully aware of them—*Secular City* became an important book. In a more formal way, Catholic theology, stimulated by Teilhard de Chardin, has already been progressively productive along these lines.

It may well be that the Hebrew Bible can be of crucial significance for the new theological movements, for it is biblical and theocentric at the same time. It speaks to the current cultural scene in ways in which neither the classical Greek heritage nor the (hitherto) orthodox Christian tradition in its dependence upon it do. For the sake of Christian theological reconstruction the Hebrew Bible may have to become basic for both the New Testament and the Christian faith. This is the setting in which we present the Hebrew Bible's account of hope and the basis for it.

II

The Hebrew Bible is a very worldly book; nevertheless, it is not a book about the world, but about the Word of God in the world. It does not pretend to give an account of the being of God; that, for the Hebrew Bible, would be the worst kind of blasphemy. God, *per se*, is an all-embracing mystery whose name can be confessed but not described, trusted but not controlled. To know God in faith is to acknowledge that one's life is lived in the keeping of this reliable mystery of power and goodness. This hidden mystery of God reveals himself by his Word in the world.

The Hebrew Bible or the Old Testament, as Christians call it, is a book about the Word of God in the world. The Word of God is always an action; it may be recalled that in Hebrew, the term for deed and word are one and the same term. The Word is the action of God in the world of man's experience; even in the case of verbal pronouncements made by prophets, their words invariably talk about something that will happen; that is, about a deed.

What is so impressive about the Hebrew Bible is its persistent concentration on the action of God in man's empirical world. God reveals himself to human experience in, through, and by means of the processes of time, space, and matter; he is always apprehended in the world even though he is not of the world. Revelation takes place in the scene of man's experience; that is what we mean when we speak of the historicity of revelation. God is not conditioned, but all apprehensions of him are. The Word of God is always an historical deed which utilizes both the impersonal processes of nature and the volitional acts of men. We must take careful note of the fact that the Bible does not set the world of man's self-assertion over against the impersonal world of nature in the manner of anthropocentric perspectives, ancient or modern. Historical revelation does not refer to that sort of distinction. Because of its theocentric perspective, the Bible draws no sharp line of distinction between impersonal natural structures and processes and acts of man's will; in every action of the Word of God both are always simultaneously operative, though perhaps in varying proportions. When we talk about historical revelation in the Bible, the antithesis we have in mind is not nature but myth. It has overcome myth by locating the Word of God in the arena of man's experience. The recrudescence of some mythical features in the cosmological dualism of apocalypticism must be viewed as an aberration, at least from the viewpoint of the Hebrew Bible and of Judaism, which persist in their worldliness.

Because of its preoccupation with the Word of God, the Hebrew Bible is theocentric; and it is worldly because it assumes that the whole meaning of the world is epitomized by its function as the scene and means for the divine action. This definition of the world and of man contains the really distinctive dimension of the biblical understanding of Creation. The world exists for the Word of God as well as by it. Creation in the Bible is not a sacral and primitive version of natural history, but an affirmation of faith about the meaning of nature. If modern biblical interpreters had always been clear about that difference, their dialogue with modern science might well have been more productive and less humiliating. "The earth is the LORD's," said the psalmist; "The world and they who dwell therein." Though the English translators have used the possessive to translate the Hebrew preposition, they could, with equal justification, have chosen the dative: man and his world are for God. He is their Creator. Creation talks about the finality of the Word of God; that is, all other meanings and functions of man and his world are subsumed under their function for God as the scene and means of his action.

The finality of the Word of God, which is the decisiveness of his action, is a constant. It extends from beginning to end, and imputes a definition of meaning to every fact, process, and purpose. That is perhaps the central thrust of the *Shema*, Israel's declaration of faith in the oneness of God. The LORD is one because this one LORD can provide everything with a significant and integrating function. In the dramatic account of the contest between the Pharaoh and the God of Israel there are ten plagues, ten progressively emphatic disclosures of the finality of the divine action. At the beginning, we are told, the magicians could match the acts of God. They too turned water into blood and made frogs come up from the Nile. But then their resources were exhausted; they were unable to duplicate the rest of the plagues. The point to this piece of artistry is that before the Word of God, all centers of authority, human and suprahuman, lose their authority and are absorbed by the one center from which all meaning ultimately proceeds. The universal finality of the action of God stands behind Israel's confession of his unity.

Though the Hebrew Bible's affirmation of the unity of God is a correlate of its confession of him as Creator, this confession, in turn, is best understood as an inference from his self-disclosure in particular human events, designated as such by those who confess him. To some extent, at least, the universality rests on particularity; the Book of Genesis was written by the community that confessed the event of Exodus. Israel was that community. Israel defines itself by the same action of God by which all creation is defined; but it does this in terms of a particular series of events that distinguish its identity and career as a human community. The definitions are mutually supportive. What is said about the universality of the Word of God is an inference from Israel's confession of itself as the people of God whose vocation is to bear witness to the reality of God's action or revelation. Israel itself, as an impirical reality in the world of time, is the primary evidence for its witness to the revealing Word of God. Without Israel the witness would collapse; it would lose its embodiment as well as its voice. Therefore Israel is an *am olam,* a people that persists as long as the age endures, because the Word of God persists in its dynamic action. Israel is God's son in the world, and lives because God does not die. To be sure, the Bible recognizes that God is not dependent upon Israel; he can choose whom he will. It is simply a mark of his faithfulness and mercy that he does not do so.

The revelation of God in his Word is told mainly as the story of a people's beginning and endurance in history, a story set in a world in which God has a covenant with Noah. Since the people defines its identity by its vocation to witness to the Word of God, its beginning and existence represent a purposeful and selective feature in the action of God. The distinctiveness of Israel is its election; and the substance of its election is its vocation to witness to the Word of God in the world.

In defining the Word of God in relation to its own experience, Israel always began with the remembrance of its own escape from slavery into freedom. This Exodus, which is the deed of God in which his authority over the human tyrant is revealed and proclaimed, is an event of rescue or redemption; the power of God is revealed in his goodness, in what theology calls grace. It must be noted, however, that God's self-revelation is by no means always expressed in deeds of redemption and grace. This is as true with respect to the events that affect Israel as with respect to those that do not. The Word of God reveals itself also in judgments that involve moral retribution and in events which, whether benign or awesome and terrible, allude to his impenetrable mystery. Particularly under the impact of prophetic preaching in Israel, the accent sometimes fell so heavily on the punitive side that the "coming of the LORD" or of the "Day of the LORD," metaphors for his self-revealing action, was viewed with alarm and dread, an emphasis that survived in apocalypticism and in Christianity. Nevertheless, in Israel the gracious goodness of God, manifest in the Exodus event, always reasserts itself; neither the disobedience of men nor the weight of the divine mystery undoes what the Word of God has done. The continuity of both Creation and Israel rests on and serves as the sign of the finality of the Word of God in its goodness.

This persistence of Israel as the Elect is always presented as a miracle of grace. To be sure, there are atempts to rationalize it: the obedience of Abraham, the intercession of Moses, the faithfulness of David, and so on. But, in the last analysis it is a matter of the integrity and faithfulness of the Word of God. He has sworn by himself, it is said. Israel disobeys and is punished. Israel suffers vicariously because she fulfills her mission in a world that is dull and obtuse; but Israel does not die. If we can imagine an ancient Israelite being challenged in modern fashion to provide evidence for his faith in the Word of God, and for his hope, he would have had a twofold answer: his people in the midst of the nations and the natural world.

The position of Israel in relation to the Word of God is a most exalted one; humanly speaking, it is indispensable. Nevertheless, it is important to take note that there is no identification of Israel as the Word of God. Israel carried the titles Elect One, Son, and Servant, titles that acquire a Christological function in the New Testament and Christianity. But in the Hebrew Bible, as applied to Israel, these titles never imply that the action of God which is his Word in the world can ever be equated with any action of Israel. The Word of God remains theocentric; it calls Israel into being and assigns its vocation; but it does not become Israel—or Exodus—in the way in which it becomes Jesus Christ. Consequently, Jesus Christ, as understood in Christianity, represents a radically novel way of talking about the Word of God; to suggest that he is, or was, simply the obedient Servant, more obedient than Israel, can thus be misleading.

In Israel the Exodus event epitomized the historical action of the Word of God; it "explained" the existence of Israel, it was the "sign" of God's rule over the nations, and Creation was an inference derived from it. If Jesus Christ were simply a new epitome of the Word of God, exemplifying new insights into its authority and finality, in relation to the human facts of sin and death, for example, the chasm between our two Bibles and two faiths would not be so great. What makes it great is the Christian identification of a particular event in the order of time, space, and matter as the very Word of God.

The simple equation of the Word of God with a particular point of coincidence in the processes of time, space, and matter constitutes the end of the world. It postulates an eschatological event that brings the action of God to an end. Nature and history are relieved of the functions they have hitherto performed for God, either because their intent has been brought to completion or because it is being realized in other ways. Actually, of course, in tradition the doctrine of the Trinity is a way of saying that for Christian faith the equation is not a simple one. It is an instance of "readjustment" noted earlier. It intends to affirm continuity with the old order on both the level of Creation and Redemption. The one God is still the creator of heaven and earth; and the dynamic action of the Holy Spirit rules the life of the new world, set in its context in the old. The Chalcedonians no doubt did the best they could in the Greek cultural setting to preserve the dynamic actuality of the Word of God, as being also in the world of time, space, and matter. But the equation of finality with the Christ-event, and its static interpretation, insured that the this-worldliness of biblical faith was impaired. Even where theocentricity was not wholly displaced by Christocentrism, the relation of the Word of God to the world came to be viewed as an indirect one. Henceforth, the meaning of the old world was redefined in the light of the new to which the scene of action had shifted. The present basis for hope, hitherto founded on the order of nature and the fact of Israel, as expressions of the Word of God, was relocated in the new age. Creation and Redemption were no longer coterminous.

III

We have stressed that Israel placed her confidence in the finality of the Word of God. By virture of its theocentricity, this action is as persistent as it is decisive. There is promise and there is fulfillment in the cycles of Israel's experience. But no fulfillment exhausts its source in the ultimate mystery. Therefore promise succeeds fulfillment, no less than preceding it. Novelty is set in the midst of continuity; it is always the old made new. The dispensationalism of apocalypticism and the Christian definition of finality, each in its own way, obscure this. They become anthropocentric and talk about a better aeon, or about a more perfect event. The purpose of God's action is very real, both in Creation and Redemption. However, despite the importance of chronology, its realization does not take the form of a progressive linear path through time. For the Old Testament *Heilsgeschichte* is not just a series of chapters in a single continued story that comes to an end in the Christ-event. It is, rather, a series of paradigmatic formulations of the perennial cycle Promise—Fulfillment. Each one is complete by itself as an illustration for the perennial faith and hope of Israel. The constancy and the continuity matter more than the progress or the goal: the ninetieth Psalm and the conclusion to the Book of Job give us some hint of Israel's own understanding of hope, complete with its characteristic features of Promise, crisis, and realization.

Israel tells the stories of creation and salvation not so much for the sake of its future, or *the* future, as for the sake of drawing attention to the present empirical reality that illustrates its faith and hope in the Word of God. The visible basis for its hope, as we have already noted, is the orderly goodness of the natural world, with its cycles of seed-time and harvest, and especially Israel itself. The ceaseless divine action binds together past, present, and future in a continuity which allows no break between time and eternity, flesh and spirit, nature and history, or Creation and Redemption. Israel is Israel because she knows this and attests it. To this day the pundits cannot agree whether Jews are best defined as a faith, a culture, or a nation. It is doubtful that they ever will. The attempts to "lift" or "reduce" the Jews to the status of a "purely spiritual community," eagerly indulged in by both liberal Christians and Reform Jews, are now dead. Less resolute attempts in the present to identify a Jew as an Israeli national won't fare any better. Israel's account of the Word of God from which she derives her self-understanding frustrates all such simplifications.

Since the natural world and Israel are the "signs" of faith in the Word of God, the Hebrew Scripture is both theocentric and "secular." This world, every part of it, serves the divine action. Therefore it is holy. One may anticipate meeting God in this world. One grasps life with both hands, as it were; one does this not simply as an act of human self-assertion, but in commitment to a religious vocation. The creation story in Genesis says about man in this respect, "Let him have dominion. . . ." The religious life, in the Hebraic sense, is the life in which man makes use of his world, exploiting it for human ends in every way he can, but remembering all the while that it is holy, i.e., that God is using it too.

The Christian theological crisis in our day is acute in proportion to the extent that the spirit of Israel's definition of the meaning of the world for man and God has embodied itself in our western civilization. In its inspiration our scientific, technological culture is Hebraic, even though its methods may be Greek. From a biblical point of view, the exploitation of the world and the manipulation of its possibilities for human purposes, whether these be material or spiritual, is a divine commandment. It points the way to a knowledge of God as well as to the realization of manhood; and it presupposes an undiminished continuity and relevance of the Word of God in the

world. The flowering of the material, temporal, and technological impulses of the Hebraic tradition in the modern world
would seem to tend to make traditional Greek formulations of
the Christian version of biblical faith uncommunicable. This
faith does speak of one God, but of two worlds; and it seems to
depreciate this world, the one modern man knows best. It appears to introduce a discontinuity into the action of God; Creation and Redemption are no longer coterminous.

We have described the official events of the so-called story
of salvation as a series of paradigmatic illustrations by means
of which the community of faith defines the meaning and result
of the Word of God at any and every point of time and experience, both in communal and personal aspects. The action of
God is always purposeful; and it always accomplishes what it
intends, by virtue of its decisiveness or finality. This we mean
to imply when we say that the theocentric action of God is
apprehended as Promise and Fulfillment. We shall conclude by
examining two of these illustrations.

The story of the Patriarchs is a piece of *Heilsgeschichte*.
There is a growing consensus that in the history of tradition it
is derivative rather than constitutive; Martin Noth, for example, describes it as an *Ausbau*. That need not concern us here,
however. For as a piece of *Heilsgeschichte*, to illustrate the
apprehension of the action of God as a perennial movement of
Promise and Fulfillment, it is complete by itself.

The Promise, in this case, is that Abraham who became a
sojourner because he heard the divine call, will become a nation, that this nation will have as its own the land in which he
is a pilgrim, and that this people, blest of God, will be a blessing to the nations.

The movement of the story is provided by the hurdles that

clutter the way to the realization of the Promise: Abraham's wife, Sarah, is barren; that is stated even before the Promise is made (Gen. 12:30). Moreover, the land is already occupied by a variety of nations. These are ready, for the most part, to accept Abraham as one of them. For example, though he does not accept it, the Hittites offer Abraham a burial place for Sarah; and later the Shechemites proposed a *connubium*. Further squabbles within his own clan threaten the Fulfillment: notably Lot and his shepherds, Esau, from whom Jacob had to flee, the treachery of Jacob's sons at Shechem and their jealousy of Joseph. Finally, famine makes flight from the promised land imperative, first for Abraham, later for Jacob, flights that further multiply the hazards.

Despite all this, the story ends as the Fulfillment of the Promise. Abraham is already a nation, seventy-five souls plus slaves, and multiplying with mysterious rapidity. His little "nation" has already been a blessing to the nations; Joseph has saved Egypt, and all the world, from famine. The world thanks God for Israel and honors it, in the Pharaoh, upon whom Jacob bestows his benediction. Wealth, honor, and communal integrity in the land of Goshen. Promise—Fulfillment. Already—not yet. That is the conclusion of every such story of salvation, including incidentally the one in the New Testament. In this case the "not yet" is illustrated by the fact that it ends in Egypt instead of in Canaan. Humanly speaking, Israel's title to the land consists only of a burial plot, purchased with money, where Sarah sleeps and to which Jacob is taken when his end comes. In the midst of Fulfillment, Promise persists.

At every point this story of salvation is told as the story of the Word of God, the action of God in, through, and by means of the processes of nature and history. The latter is represented by such items as Lot's economic opportunism, Sarah's attempt to make the promise come true by using Hagar, and the hatred of Jacob's sons for the rather insufferable Joseph. Fulfillment in spite of history but, nevertheless, by means of it: "You meant it for evil, but God meant it for good" is the summary of the matter. Also with respect to nature, the story is simultaneously radically theocentric and this-worldly. Many migrated along the Fertile Crescent from the east, to end up in Haran or Canaan; but only Abraham went by divine command. In times of famine, Asiatic tribes traditionally went to Egypt and Ishmaelites sold many slaves; what is noted in this story is the divine action, not the natural and cultural means. Finally, Isaac is portrayed a child of God's promise; a gift, nevertheless, in the natural order. And the rite of circumcision ties together the theocentricity and finality of the Word of God with the continuity of its action in the world. Abraham believed God and obeyed him, even though the very realization of the promise was in jeopardy in his act of obedience. But the elect one does not die. That is, the Binding of Isaac announces that Israel lives in the world wholly at his disposal. But it is the will of God that he live in the world. As such, along with Creation in nature, Israel is the empirical basis for hope. The typological treatment of the *Akedah* has obscured the most important aspects of the meaning of hope in the Old Testament.

We shall deal very briefly with the second paradigmatic illustration of Israel's faith that the Word of God is always apprehended as Promise—Fulfillment. This is the story of Exodus. Its setting is in the arena of political power; its special theme is the finality of the divine action with respect to the human tyrant and whatever demonic forces may be at his disposal. The story is unquestionably one, most probably *the* one,

that lies at the heart of Israel's tradition and is constitutive of
it.

On its dramatic side the story unfolds the finality of the
divine action. The Pharaoh who, at the outset, asks "Who is
the LORD?" discovers, step by step, that he is the center of
power who has all other powers at his disposal, whether of
nature, gods, demons, or men. The several attempts in the
course of the ten plagues to strike a compromise agreement
come to nothing, at bottom because God's rule is not divisible.
The radical theocentricity is again apparent; the action is by
means of the world of nature and men, but the meaning of all
of these is in the purpose they serve, whether wittingly or un-
wittingly.

The story stresses the servanthood of Moses, the helplessness
of the slaves, and their quiescence. Israel, sometimes an active
participant in the divine action, as in the Holy War of Joshua,
is here a mere pawn in a contest of power between the Lord
and the historical tyrant. Partly because of this and partly because it reports a rescue of the elect, the story may be
said to lie in the order of Redemption.

In the case of the Patriarchs the accent fell on the Promise;
the indications of Fulfillment were more casual. With the Exodus story, the situation is reversed. The Promise is implicit:
these are the people of Abraham. That explains their fertility,
which the stupid ruler of Egypt both fears and underestimates.
It also implies that they do not belong in Egypt and are bound
for the land promised to their fathers. The Fulfillment is fea-
tured. The destruction of the Egyptian army at the sea, even
more than the death of the first-born, carries the note of finality: "the Egyptians whom you see today you will never see
again" (Ex. 14:13), Moses assures the fearful Israelites at the

sea. And, at the conclusion of the Song of Moses in the next chapter we read "the LORD will reign forever and ever," a line immortalized by Handel's *Messiah*. Moreover, Israel's calendar is said to take its chronological sequence from this event. Nevertheless the finality lies in the action of God rather than in the event or in the people who are rescued. The fulfillment is, as always, one in which the "Already" is immediately superseded by the awareness of the "Not yet." Moreover, the decisiveness of the action does not mark the attainment of a static end or goal but serves as an assurance of its continuance.

Finality reactivates Promise. Hope is possible because of the inexhaustible mystery of the dynamic Word of God. The continuity of nature and that of the people of God exemplify this mystery. The world is one because God is one. It continues to serve his purpose, in Creation and in Redemption, for these remain coterminous.

EUGENE B. BOROWITZ

Hope Jewish and Hope Secular

Representing one of the major religious traditions which confess belief in the future of man, RABBI EUGENE B. BOROWITZ approaches the topic from the position of "Hope Jewish and Hope Secular." He speaks for American Reform Judaism out of an exceptionally broad and rich theological experience as teacher, scholar, lecturer, and author. Teaching appointments at Hebrew Union College, New York; at Jewish Theological Seminary of America; at Princeton, Temple, and Columbia Universities; and lectures throughout the United States and abroad are indicators of Rabbi Borowitz's extraordinarily deep and abiding concern and prolific thought.

He is the author of *A Layman's Introduction to Religious Existentialism* (Philadelphia: Westminster, 1965); a contributor to *Rediscovering Judaism,* ed. A. J. Wolf (Chicago: Quadrangle, 1965); to *Great Jewish Ideas,* ed. A. E. Millgram (New York: Taplinger, 1966); to *The Meaning of the Death of God,* ed. Bernard Murchland (New York: Random House, 1967); and is editor of *The Jewish Sources Speak* (New York: B'nai B'rith [Taplinger]). He also contributes an annual review of books in the fields of theology and philosophy of religion to the Central Conference of American Rabbis' *Journal,* and for several years he wrote a column on contemporary theological literature for the quarterly, *Judaism.*

THE WORK of Jewish theology today, as I understand it, must be carried out from a post-secular stance. Because that position determines the view of hope offered here, some preliminary remarks concerning it are required.

With the emancipation of the Jews from ghetto existence, beginning at about the end of the eighteenth century, Judaism underwent a steady process of secularization, in the contemporary, limited sense of that term. On one level this process was associated with the radical change in the political status of the Jews. Only with the emergence of a secular, as contrasted to a Christian, state was it possible for Jews to have full rights as citizens. The Jews therefore welcomed the secular state in Western Europe and avidly took advantage of its new opportunities for civic participation. Such a state implied the acceptance of a certain neutral, religion-free area of existence. This basic political secularization was amplified by the urban concentration of Jews and by their speedy movement into the universities wherever this was permitted. As the nineteenth century advanced, this process moved toward self-consciousness. Traditional Judaism saw the need to explain itself to the surrounding world. Or, what is the same thing, having adopted the style of the general society, it now had to explain itself to itself in that society's terms. This meant using the language of secular philosophy to talk about Judaism. While German idealism was more hospitable to religious interpretation than contemporary secular philosophy, the very process of employing a philosophic hermeneutic made its demands for the transformation of Judaism. These social and intellectual pressures were so great that when Orthodox Judaism emerges in the person of Samson Raphael Hirsch, it—as well as Reform Judaism—appears as a self-consciously "religious" movement and thus, as contrasted to the older synthesis of folk and faith, one touched by the modern secular spirit. The effects were internal as well. Among the Reform Jews the service was translated into the vernacular, the legal disciplines were reduced to subjectively desirable norms and the clergy lost its aura of infallibility. Yet even among the traditionalists the observance of Jewish civil law speedily gave way to the use of the governments' courts, and general as well as Jewish education became acceptable— both unthinkable concepts a century before. The decades have only increased this involvement with secularity.

The process took a more radical turn on the part of those Jews who felt that modernity meant some sort of scientific or materialistic positivism. By the last quarter of the nineteenth century many Jewish intellectuals knew that God was dead and religion was hopelessly outmoded. They wrote about it, preached it and organized in terms of it. Their substitutes for Jewish faith, which were very much felt in the Jewish world, took the form of socialism, if they were determined to transcend their Jewishness, or Zionist nationalism, if they were proud of it, or socialist Zionism, if they wanted the best of both worlds. They demythologized Jewish religious concepts into politics. The prophets were agitators for social justice. *Galut*, "exile," was a matter of political geography rather than of metaphysical alienation of God and man in this world. *G'ulah*, "redemption," they took back to its early sense of reacquiring one's family land instead of meaning equally the establishing of the Messianic Kingdom. The State of Israel is the fulfillment of that secularization of Judaism.

In the United States these European activities came much later, mass migration being a late nineteenth- and early twentieth-century phenomenon, and they were transformed by the special social situation of an open and expanding society. Its early and perhaps characteristic example was the establishment of the Ethical Culture movement by a Jew. A large number of Jews at once flocked to it as a perfect synthesis of the non-sacred in Judaism with the moral in democracy. Today it would seem that the high point of American Jewish secularization was reached just before World War II. There were by then enough native-born Jews and aspiring young immigrants in the universities or involved in the general, secular culture for them to have a positive intellectual inducement to give up their ancestral religion. What gave that movement tremendous force in the Jewish community was its link to the psycho-social pressures generated by the cultural distance between the immigrant Yiddish-speaking older generation and their American-oriented children. For Jewish youth Americanization meant non-observance of Jewish law, sophistication meant atheism. Statistically these may not have been the majority style, yet they were widespread, well-known and much worried-over. No wonder that spokesmen for Judaism in this period were seeking secular syntheses by elaborating a naturalist—that is, functional, non-metaphysical—explanation of Jewish faith, as was Mordecai Kaplan, or by experimenting with other, even less God-oriented, forms of humanism.

Anyone who lived through these past few decades of American Jewish history, or who because of his own struggle has vicariously made his own the century-and-a-half difficulties of the Jewish community since the Emancipation began—and it is not yet nearly complete—cannot help but marvel at the revolution which the discovery of the secular realm has apparently begun in both Protestant and Catholic circles. We always thought the church was in the world and part of culture while we were still emerging. Now we wonder what kind of spiritual ghetto it is from which Christianity seeks emancipation. Usually Jews borrow theological patterns from their neighbors. For a change a theological movement seems to have passed through Judaism before reaching Christianity. Almost certainly this is because we are structured as a folk or a people and not as a church. We could not therefore, even in pre-Emancipation days, be as separate from the secular as Christians have felt themselves to be.

From these decades of experience with secularity it is part sad, part astonishing, to hear it being welcomed as a religious aid of messianic proportions. Of course we must all understand and in part accommodate ourselves to contemporary secularity. Of course we must speak to modern man in a modern way. But our experience is that translating the service makes it not only understandable but also unbelievable to many; turning law into a matter of individual decision leads not only to willing compliance but gross non-observance, almost to anarchy; and humanizing the authorities makes them not only more approachable but less influential in most people's lives. A religious concern with the secular style of our time may solve some of our older pressing problems and so may be necessary. But it will also lose us many of the old values we have treasured and create new problems which will then demand newer solutions. That is what brings us to the post-secular stance.

Since World War II the Jewish community seems to have rounded a theological corner, at least in some small minority of its members. I do not refer now to the unexpectedly high proportion of Jews who affiliate with synagogues, who have built an incredibly large number of beautiful religious buildings and who in some measure participate in their activities.

While no observer of American Jewish life in the late '30's could have expected it, such a return today seems more often a new way of secularizing Judaism than a genuine religious movement. Even more unexpected and important is that small group who, having come through atheism or socialism or ideological Zionism or pure secularist indifference, are now seriously seeking the meaning of Jewish faith. On the intellectual level it is an interdenominational—*mirabile dictu*—group of theologians and rabbis who are trying to go beyond Buber and Rosenzweig in the search for a new sense of Covenant, law and community. They dominated the under-fifty group in the Commentary symposium *On the Condition of Jewish Belief*. They find themselves met in every Jewish community they visit by a small but thoughtful group who are anxious to hear about Jewish belief, and the more existentially challenging the presentation the better they like it. They are not many, but that they exist at all, that they care as they do, is what provides the social reality to this post-secular stance of Jewish theology. In concern, if not yet in theological substance, they know why they are Jewish. By contrast, why should one who takes secularity seriously care about his Jewishness? Ethics are universal; psychic needs are for doctors to treat or experiences to fill; belonging is supplied by Americanism, ethnic enrichment by folk music or crafts, imported from the whole world; culture is forced on him by a booming culture industry. So a large number of Jews are too secular to take Judaism or even Jewishness seriously, yet have too much self-respect to surrender them entirely. That is what the alliance with secularity has brought us to and that is why, living with it for years now, I approach the analysis of modern man's sense of hope in the future not uncritically.

There can be little doubt that all of us today are very much concerned with what is new, with what is coming to be. On a vulgar level much of our economy is based on it. The annual change in automobile models sets a tone which the manufacturers of appliances, clothing and other products seek to emulate. We engineer for obsolescence. We are equally concerned with the novel in our social styles, looking for the new restaurant, resort or thing to do. And our omnipresent communications media put their great energy into what they know will sell, the sensational and the different.

That is the superficial side of what technology and history have taught us. Invention has demonstrated again and again that things need not be what they were. Looking back over the ages, the men we most admire are the innovators who have improved man's condition or broadened the horizons of his spirit. Those movements have not stopped. That good future we would like is even now coming into being. Today is even now becoming "the old days."

There is much in this modern mood about which religion and the contemporary secular spirit can agree. Both are discontented with the present situation of man and society. They know things are not what they ought to be and that it is critical for man to devote himself to making them better. Secular man proposes to do so by what we may call horizontal transcendence. By projecting human creativity forward through time he hopes to overcome the present problems. There is, in all logical rigor, no present evidence that such a positive outcome is possible. All we can see is difficulties, false solutions and creative discontent. We do have some experience of such problems having been met in the past. Still that says nothing in principle about these. So even in secular hope there is also a certain measure of faith, a commitment that goes beyond the present evidence and is strong enough to build one's life upon.

Here too religious men and those of a secular temper can meet, for this horizontal conception of hope is clearly to be seen in the Bible. The major Hebrew term for hope, *k-v-ḥ*, means in the Bible not just a state of soul but an expectation in time. The dictionaries often give its meaning as "to wait for." Hope in God is the trust one has in one's present distress that God will soon act to bring him relief. That temporal sense of hope is reinforced by the frequent parallelism of terms from the root *k-v-ḥ* with those from *y-ḥ-l*, which far more specifically means to await or look for. Another root, similarly but less frequently used in these contexts, *ḥ-k-h*, even more concretely denotes temporal expectation. Much has been written about the historical orientation of biblical faith, and this is surely a striking corroboration of it. Our most natural inclination today would be to think of hope as something inner, emotional, essentially subjective. Yet for the Bible it is quite objectively connected with events to take place in time. Moreover, where we would assume that hope was primarily for the self or perhaps for his loved ones, in the Bible it is as much a concern for the community, the people of Israel, as it is for the individual. When the Hebrews express their folk distress and hope in God they say they wait for him, which means they wait for him to make himself felt in history on their behalf. That sense of communal hope is one of the most common prophetic and psalmic themes. And the individual and corporate levels do not contradict each other. Rather they seem to complement each other. Thus very often it is difficult to tell in the Psalms whether the usage, though expressed individually, is not meant communally. On occasion a clear-cut community usage suddenly slips into the first person, or vice versa. In biblical times individual and people were not nearly as separate as they are today when subjective autonomy and individualism are methodological necessities. In ancient time self and folk merged, the one into the other.

That may help us understand why even personally there was such a strong sense of temporal hope in Biblical Judaism. The major historic event it knew and celebrated was the Exodus from Egypt. That experience of God's helping power seems to have been as dominant a motif of Jewish faith as anything we find in the biblical experience. God had brought the people forth from slavery and given them a law and a land. He became the Hebrews' God by overcoming a tragic historic situation and turning it into one of fulfillment. No matter how many tribes actually participated, the Exodus became the major religious memory of all the people of Israel. So it could be their hope that he would do so again and again for them in history. The individual Hebrew, one may surmise, by participating in his people's sense of having a saving God, came to understand the experience of his own life in similar bondage-transcending, exodus-granting terms. He, too, could hope that God would act on his behalf in the situation in which he found himself. Both levels of expectation—that people and individual alike would find God working on their behalf to bring them out of their trouble—were confirmed by experience. That does not mean God always gave them prosperity and success. They had the capacity to see him working for their benefit even in what would otherwise have appeared as defeat or disaster. Perhaps that is why they did not lose their faith in his active presence in history when it might seem he had deserted them. Their trust that he would yet act, for individuals

and community alike, was often strained, and they expressed
their feelings to their God in terms of desperation. Yet it held
fast through centuries of trial, and every new exodus-
experience now made the old Egypt events the faithful paradigm of God's living, active relationship with his people and
each of its members.

That sense of God's present power in history is a major
ingredient in the Hebrew understanding that the relationship
with God is best symbolized by the concept of Covenant.
God's responsibility in that relationship is, among other things,
to save his people. One might then say that because the people
of Israel have a Covenant with God, they can hope that he will
act for them in history. That describes it in fairly clear biblical
terms, though I think the religious reality is better put this
way: because the people of Israel knew their God to work on
their behalf in history they could use the juridic concept of
Covenant to symbolize their relationship with him.

What is critical from the point of view of our modern theological problematic is the dialectic sense of action under the
Covenant. Because God is expected to act does not mean that
man may now do nothing and simply wait. The Hebrews must
walk themselves out of Egypt though they know they were
borne on eagles' wings. The Hebrew judges and kings must
lead their armies into battle even though they have been told the
Lord will fight for them. To be sure, God occasionally takes
quite independent action in the form of a miracle. That is his
free right as sovereign Lord. Yet the law forbids testing him in
this regard, and waiting for his help therefore does not mean
giving up trust in what men must yet do. Only when everything
has been done does one wait for a miracle.

The human side of the Covenant dialectic of action is, as

befits man's stature in contrast to God's, far more limited. For man to act simply on his own—that is to say, without regard for his Covenant partner—is always wrong. It may seem to lead to success, but it is nonetheless sin and will be met with punishment. Man's action is truly significant only when it takes place in accordance with God's will. Since he is sovereign in history, such acts can endure and bring blessing. More, when a man does them, he knows he does them with God's help, for that is the direction in which God himself is moving history. The act is now quite precisely a Covenant act in which man and God join together to do a deed, yet each remains himself in his own integrity. On the common, everyday level, Jewish hope is the hope that God is joining us in what we are doing, that we are doing acts in which God can act with us. That sense of Covenant partnership in the deeds of every day is in principle no different from its more dramatic manifestation. In moments of danger, personal or communal, we trust that God will act on our behalf. Here too it is normally men who must petition, appeal, fight or go into exile. Yet we know our acts mean nothing without his help. The pious, however, have realized that that was equally true of every act we did in calmer and more quiet days.

This Covenant dialectic of man and God linked to one another in any meaningful historical activity is to be found almost everywhere in the Bible. Eventually and inevitably, so it would seem, it leads onto a third level of hope—that God will use his saving power in such a way that there will be, so to speak, no more need for him to act again. One day there will be an ultimate exodus from the human slaveries that men call history and an entrance into the promised land of God's rule and man's full-hearted obedience. That dream of Hebrew

eschatology is quite difficult to trace in its genesis and historical development. Shall the prophetic symbols for the age to
come be taken rather literally to counteract the unwarranted
spiritualization of their writings by generations of homileti-
cians? Or shall they be understood in symbolic depth, using the
human language of a given time and place to express a truth
that here as elsewhere transcends its environment? Shall we
say that the prophets before the Exile only spoke of doom and
not of hope; or, if reproof without hope seems unreasonable,
then how much hope may an early voice be permitted to have
in a non-Hegelian world? And how shall we determine the
criteria by which we choose the criteria by which to give our
answers?

What can safely be said in the face of these problems is that
Biblical Judaism came eventually to contain an eschatological
level to its hope, and that seems perfectly in keeping with its
sense of the Covenant between God and Israel. If God is truly
sovereign over the creation and concerned that his will be
done among men, if he repeatedly acts to make this happen
and covenants with Israel to bring it about, then it seems rea-
sonable that in due course he should see to it that this effort
reaches a proper conclusion. That alone is commensurate with
his sole rule as God. It also reinforces, and is in turn strength-
ened by, the individual and folk levels of biblical faith. Every
saving act on the personal or communal level substantiated the
faith that God's Kingdom would one day come on earth. And
when the individual or the people of Israel verged on despair,
they were buoyed by the knowledge that any defeat they might
now suffer could not impede God's, and therefore Israel's, ultimate triumph in history.

Jews have always been incredulous when they have been

told that Israel's Covenant and its eschatological hope are contradictory, that only by its Covenant being broken or superseded could its messianic visions be fulfilled. Jews today remain no less unconvinced. If anything, they are somewhat astonished that so archaic an attitude, so pre-Conciliar a point of view, can still be heard in serious scholarly circles. Were the Exilic and post-Exilic prophets of the Bible not truly God's prophets when they called for the reestablishment of the Temple, the observance of Jewish law, and affirmed the eternity of Israel's relationship to God? Was the Jewish people which heard the prophets, preserved their writings and transmitted their message in unbroken tradition over the centuries, completely misled and deluded? Even more important, has the community of Israel throughout the ages, indeed is the Household of Israel today, not God's people, not truly bound to him in a Covenant as real and as effective today as when it was made at Sinai? Any such imputation that there can be no living religious reality to Israel's presence in the world today, or that there cannot be any integrity to its structure of hope, must be rejected as blind to the reality of biblical faith and its living manifestation in Jewish lives both today and through the ages.

Regardless of the origins of Jewish eschatology, it was by the early centuries of our common era as fundamental to Jewish hope as was God's trustworthiness toward individuals and the people as a whole. It is true that some rabbis speak of the messianic era in quite naturalistic terms while others give a miraculous interpretation. Often that spectrum of opinion exists because of a distinction between a naturalistic messianic time which is only the prelude to the trans-naturalistic Kingdom of God himself, though this usage is not consistent. The rabbis, although they did not encourage such anti-historical

speculation, yet allowed great individual freedom in these
ruminations. They could do so because they firmly fixed eschatological as well as personal and communal hope into the pattern of Jewish observance. It is a leading motif of the *kaddish*
doxology, is found in four of the last five of the regular petitions of the daily service, and is the major theme of the New
Year's and Day of Atonement liturgy. Indeed the place where
the word *hope* figures most prominently in Jewish liturgy is the
original New Year's prayer for the establishment of God's
kingdom which for about six centuries now has been closing
every Jewish service. Its second paragraph begins, "We therefore hope in Thee, O Lord our God, that we may speedily
behold the glory of thy might, when Thou wilt remove idols
from the earth and the non-gods shall be utterly destroyed,
when Thou shalt establish the world as The Kingdom of God
. . ." And one can see the eschatological dimension of Jewish
hope intertwined with the individual and folk concerns in the
opening paragraph of the petitions recited at least three times
each day. The mighty God who yet helped one man, Abraham,
is now addressed as he who will bring a Redeemer to save all
the Household of Israel.

This brief survey should be sufficient to indicate why that
old Jewish hope is unacceptable to modern secular man.
Though Biblical Judaism too knows dissatisfaction with the
present and has faith that it will be transcended in time to
come, it affirms this horizontal trust because it knows a vertical
reality. It believes the present can be transcended because it
believes in a transcendent God. Here the paths diverge. Secular man, by popular definition, knows no transcendent reality.
His hope for the future is in the enhancement of man's capabil-
ities. With the improved techniques and knowledge time will

bring, man will be able to overcome problems which are not now soluble. That represents only faith in man and his capacities—perhaps, too, a trust in nature's accommodation to man or a feeling that to change things may change the quality of existence. All these may still be called horizontal factors.

That is what makes Marxism such an interesting case in the contemporary secular world. At one time a Marxist view of society and history might well seem to qualify as the height of secularity. Today our secularity is too radical for such a judgment. Marxism still bears the genetic signs of its idealistic parentage, for it retains a sense of transcendence even though it has sought to stand the Hegelian dialectic on materialistic feet. The classic Marxist believes that there is at work in and through human history a process which will inevitably bring about the socialist state or some other such messianic surrogate. It would be wisest for men to identify and cooperate with this inevitable development, but even if they do not, it will surely come to be. What powers this hope is its recognition of a process beyond man's ultimate control that moves history to a predetermined end. It may be located in nature and closely identified with economic structures and dynamics. But insofar as it is beyond deflection or control, it is in the category of transcendent realities. Moreover, since it is inaccessible to test or verification, yet explains everything, it seems in Marx's own sense an ideology, and a religious one at that. There may be great virtue in creating dialogues with Marxists today, particularly in Europe; yet that has little to do with the problem of interpreting religion to secular man. Because he rejects all transcendence and ideological formulation for his tentative commitments and pragmatic understandings he is essentially post-Marxist with regard to history even where he uses Marx's sociology, and that seems increasingly true in Europe, as in the United States. Indeed one cannot help but wonder if it is not a recognition of its failing intellectual appeal that makes Marxism open to discussion with religion.

The fundamental question, then, between secularists and biblical religions is, To what extent is hope possible without faith in a transcendent reality? Are the problems of human existence ones which are in principle within human competence to resolve, or must the future inevitably involve men in the same fundamental human difficulties? Suppose that by the elaboration of medical techniques men could have great stretches of time—perhaps even endlessly extended—and the vigor to use it. Would that answer the problem of self-fulfillment? If being a man implies a sense of intellectual, esthetic and, more particularly, moral excellence, if it implies dissatisfaction with anything less than a fully integrated self in spirit and in action, man's problem is not time or technique but the distance between finite self and infinite aspiration. His problem lies in the quality of existence, and while he may modify it he cannot change it. Even endless time could only bring man to despair, for with many years and undreamed-of help he still could not live in the fullness he knows he ought to reach. Even without death to dramatize his limits, endless time itself could only bring him an endless sense of ultimate frustration.

If that is man's existential reality, it would be absurd for him to face the future with an attitude so fundamentally positive as to be worthy of the term hope. It is even more difficult to believe, except by some quixotic self-assertion against the universe, that he could in some secular fashion make hope the fundamental principle of his existence. As I see it, modern man's trust in the future must necessarily be self-contradictory. If we know nothing which can radically change the present, then the future can only mollify or alleviate our existential discontent. As important and as useful as that may be, that sentiment hardly qualifies as hope. If we know that the years to come will be essentially as disquieting as now, though with some improvements and conveniences, then our attitude toward them may be expectation, anticipation, desire or longing but is something quite distinct from the old religious virtue hope. I believe a fresh look at modern man's continual concern with what is yet to be will show this, in fact, to be the case.

We have, however, come to a fundamental methodological problem, one which is insoluble, yet unavoidable. Out of the plethora of evidence available, how do we know exactly what the secular mentality is? How can we be certain that we are talking about modern man rather than our fantasies concerning him? Since he is considered scientifically-oriented, one would think that empirical factors would be critical. Yet, as in the death-of-God dispute, we ignore such statistical data as exists since we assume that most people are really behind the times. In talking of secular man, then, theologians are playing at spiritual sociology. I suppose the only way we shall know who is right is by applying one biblical standard for prophecy and waiting to see whether things turn out as predicted. In the meantime the best any such speculation can do is to provide a useful hermeneutic for understanding some of the movements in our society, though just which ones and how many one cannot say. I would suggest, as one handy rule for understanding such analysis, that we tend to find the significantly new in reaction to what we are tired of seeing.

Again Hegel refuses to die. In the interpretation which follows I admit my amateur standing as a social diagnostician and confess that if there is anything I am overly acquainted with it is Jewish secularity usurping Jewish religiousness.

I see modern man's concern for the future as quite spurious, a rationalization or an escape, but not a genuine hope. On one level I believe this is true because in substantial part we have had the experience of reaching a hoped-for future and finding it wanting. American society has made a tremendous leap forward in the past two decades. Many, many people today—unfortunately not all—have had an entirely unexpected number of their fondest dreams fulfilled. Our cars, clothes, homes, appliances, vacations, recreation, are often far better than ever could have been imagined twenty years ago. Then we believed that if only we had this or that, we would be happy. Now we have been given much of what we asked—and it has not solved anything. We do not want to go back to life as it was, but we have learned—decisively, I think—that having is not being. We still want more and better things only because the present might be better, not because we can any longer have genuine hope in the future. The disappointment that has come to communists with the achievement of communist states is a commonplace of the post-modern world.

That explains why we are less oriented to the future than we are to the present. The most obvious economic fact of our times is not that people invest but that they live on credit, that they mortgage their futures to pay for pleasures now. They do so because they do not trust in the future as much as did their parents. They cannot be certain they will ever get there, so everyone is on a pleasure spree seeking to fill the now with the justification of existence. The squares experiment with restaurants and travel, the liberals with sex and the radicals with drugs. Even the multi-media dance halls are no voyage into the future, only a non-pharmaceutical way of blotting out time by overloading the senses. I cannot see how we can ignore this massive redirection from the future to the present, nor do I see what else can explain it but our lack of faith in the future.

On a far more intellectual level Albert Camus had seen this in the early 1940's. In his novel *The Plague* and elsewhere he characterized modern man as one who must learn to live without hope. If he is, by definition, a man who sacrifices all illusion to face reality, then the most dangerous illusion of all, the one he must therefore most thoroughly surrender, is hope. Camus knew that without some transcendent standard or reality the future could be no better than the past, and he also knew that transcendence was no longer accessible. Being as humane as he was honest, he asked how man could now keep from despair—and, most radically, suicide—how he might come to exercise common decency toward others. He failed to validate ethics without transcendence, yet his quest remains the productive model for courageous secularity.

I have presented these three aspects of the modern experience not only to argue that it is not essentially future-oriented but equally to remind us of its radical rejection of transcendence. If our apologetic strategy leads us to the attempt to explain religious hope in secular terms, we must inevitably compromise the fundamental nature of the biblical trust. The secular concern for the future, and indeed its current escape into the present, does afford us an opportunity to speak of similar dissatisfactions which must similarly be met by faith. Still at some point our apologetics must give way to a certain polemical thrust no matter in how friendly or open a way it is set forward. Surely no dialogue is worth entering into if one cannot stand one's own ground in full and equal dignity.

The strange fate of hope in modern Jewish history is worthy of special consideration in this regard. The old tri-partite structure of biblical hope—personal, communal, and eschatological—held together, with some variety in the configuration, throughout the Middle Ages. Apart from individual influences, such as that of Spinoza, it remained for the concept of autonomy created by the Enlightenment, systematically elaborated by Kant and given special power by the secular state and modern science, to bring about major reconsideration and change. Validation now meant personal experience, rational, moral or religious. Eschatology was the primary victim of this process, for what could the individual personally know of what waited beyond historic times? The folk hope somehow managed to survive, though how personal evidence could provide a mandate for group existence remained an unsolved problem which continues to disturb Jewish theology even in the present, more rigorously individualistic, time. Hope for man survived, since that was the dogmatic foundation of the concept of autonomy. If the Jewish people helped individuals and even mankind, then one might hope that it would survive in history.

The Holocaust under Hitler destroyed that liberal reconstruction and yet prevented a return to the traditional modes of belief. It was no longer possible to make the goodness of man the cornerstone of Jewish faith. Yet who could see God acting in this horror-filled history? That is not because it was traumatic. The Jewish people had been able to see God in disaster before. The prophetic interpretation of the biblical catastrophes had long since set the standard which the Jews utilized to explain disasters as substantial as the destruction of the Second Temple, the defeat of Bar Kochba, the expulsion from Spain, the rampage of Chmelnicki. None had caused a break with the Jewish tradition of hope though it had often been reinterpreted. Now, however, the social suffering was too great to be seen as any sort of divine punishment or instruction. And the pain of endless individuals was too great to find explanation in the survival of the people or in such eschatological promises as might still be extended. If God did not act for individuals and Israel, how could one hope he would ever act again? How could one even trust that he was there?

It is characteristic of Judaism that if any new statement of atheism was to move the Jewish community after World War II it had to come on the basis of what happened in history rather than because philosophers worry about whether statements about God can have significant intellectual content. Jews, for all their intellectuality, do not seem so rationalistic as to find in the arguments of philosophy a compelling reason for saying that God is dead. On the other hand, they have been amazed that the major death-of-God thinkers have not discussed the unparalleled destruction of Jews under Hitler as a reason for disbelief in God. Yet that alone has agitated the Jewish community whenever it sought to speak of the Jewish faith.

That social interpretation is, of course, subjective, but I think it is quite widespread. But now we come to the problem of reading the social evidence on an even more significant level. How does one know that this, and not that, event is revelatory? Why did the Hebrews say it was the Exodus and Sinai and not the four-hundred-year slavery or the Golden Calf which taught them what was finally true and ultimately real? I do not know the answer to those questions. I only know that for me, and I believe for the Jewish people as a whole, the Holocaust was shattering but not determinative. It was not the Sinai of our time. It burned us, tortured us, scarred us, and does so still today. Nonetheless, its obscene brutality did not become our paradigm for future history. I have never been able to cease wondering, in the technical, biblical sense, at the fact that after the Holocaust there was no mass desertion of Judaism. If anything, there arose in the community as a whole a conscious desire to reclaim and reestablish Jewish existence. It was no more than that. Yet, considering what Jewishness had just entailed, that spontaneous inner reassertion was uncanny. It testified to what surpasses man's wisdom and courage and yet sustains and carries him through the terrors of personal and social history. I find it also significant (though of lesser significance) that today, despite substantial publicity to a community generally recognized as highly secularized, the Jewish death-of-God movement has found very little acceptance. I attribute this to the social fact that while to others religious atheism sounds new and radical, to us it is somehow very old-fashioned. Atheism is where we all were in the '30's and the '40's, in the days when we still thought university rationalism would redeem the world. That is what those of us who still care about Judaism deliberately turned from, so to revive it now for a new Judaism seems strangely behind the times. What is more important, the very phenomenon it should explain to us it destroys instead. For to say that there is no God means saying that everything is permissible. The Holocaust, explained in these terms, is neutralized, robbed of its negative force. For then by what right are we disgusted, nauseated, overwhelmed, outraged at what happened to the innocent, if the event is seen only as an honest reflection of reality and not as an intolerable violation of right inherent in the universe itself? The new atheism would rob us of our moral indignation, and it is just that which the Jewish community knows better than to surrender. Some decades back, it could be tolerant of an atheism which left ethics standing. Today secular ethics is a vanishing myth and atheism means nihilism. That is to lose the very moral ground from which the protest against God was launched.

Post-Holocaust Jewish theology found itself in a period where only a negative methodology might be intellectually bearable, though hardly emotionally effective. Any effort to explain the Holocaust would by that very fact betray the event and our reactions to it. So nothing could be said. Yet unbelief was equally impossible because of the moral affirmation inherent in the very protest. We could not speak, but we could not not believe. We could only have a theology of non-nonbelief. That was not much, but it was more than nothing. Considering what we had been through, considering that some of us had been through it and refused not to believe, that would have been the realistic content of Jewish hope in history.

Now, once again, historic events have shaken us to our foundations. I cannot discuss Jewish hope today without discussing the June 1967 Arab-Israeli war. Permit me to remind you of my biblical frame of reference. Hope for the individual Jew was until recent times intimately linked with the fate of his people, and what happened to the Jewish people in history affected the individual Jew's sense of personal hope insofar as it was founded on Jewish faith. That personal-communal relationship stems from Israel's Covenant with God. The individual Jew shares God's Covenant as one of the people of Israel, and that means that he is by divine act tied to all Jews everywhere in the world, especially those who live in the Land of Israel, and his destiny is necessarily linked with theirs. That ethnic closeness in a religious faith may be more than one

normally expects in a church, but God called the children of
Israel to him as a folk and not as a church. That social structure has over the ages been found fully appropriate to its purpose of endurance through history.

Jewish hope, moreover, is linked to what God does in historic time. If the Jews find themselves in a house of bondage,
they await God's saving action in the here and now. That was
the trauma of the Holocaust. So if we are to speak of Jewish
hope, then we must speak of the fate of the Jews, and in our
times that means among other communities quite specifically the
State of Israel. That sounds like politics to many Christians
and hence strangely unreligious. But Christian categories will
not do here. The destiny of the Household of Israel is a theo-
political matter now as it was in biblical times. Neither man's
institutions for channeling governmental power nor God's
concern with what this people must yet do in history can be
eliminated when discussing the Jews and their Judaism.

That Monday afternoon when the war began and no news
of what was taking place came through, there was black anxiety throughout the Jewish world. The question was not military—who would win. It was theological. Would God abandon the people of Israel again and allow the citizens of the
State of Israel to be slaughtered by Arab armies? For weeks we
had heard of Radio Cairo's threats to exterminate the Jews of
the State of Israel and we had watched as the mobs there and
in other Arab capitals were whipped into a frenzied hatred of
the Israelis. We knew the danger was real and not exaggerated,
that if the Arab armies drove back the Israelis there would be
an incredible massacre which the Western governments would
not intercede in time to stop. And God had shown us already
once in this century that he could withdraw from history suffi-

ciently to allow his people to be slaughtered. Could we survive another holocaust? It was not, then, only the Israeli armies who were on trial that day but, in very earnest, God himself.

Then came the victory, clean, sharp and decisive; gained by intelligence and skill backed by moral will and determination; unsullied by brutality, vengefulness, atrocity or vindictiveness. We sophisticates thought we knew historical reality and therefore had discounted much of the Bible. Now, before our very eyes, history turned biblical once again. Of course it was relief, elation—a victory at last and a great one. That only begins the explanation, for the truth is that to our own surprise we sensed the presence of a transcendent reality operating in history that we had almost come to believe could no longer make itself felt there. We knew all the technical reasons for the Israeli success, but we also knew they did not explain what had happened. Without soldiers and generals, without equipment and training, nothing could have happened. But what happened was more than what they alone could do, and so we naturally and necessarily gave thanks to Him who works wonders and delivers His people from Egypt. We saw Him once again as He who remembers His Covenant. I am not saying that the Israeli victory proves to Jews that there is a God. I am saying that what happened in June spoke to us in a way that, for example, the Sinai campaign of 1956 did not. For a moment the tight, naturalistic structure through which we secularized men see everything cracked open and we saw Him. So we cannot speak of Jewish hope today as we would have done after the Holocaust but before the war.

You will have noticed that I have not spoken of what happened to them, there in the State of Israel, but of what happened to us. This was of course their politics, their war and their immediate suffering. But while we are not bound to them politically, we were by virtue of being one people under God intimately involved in their crisis. How could we who have been through this Holocaust and post-Holocaust era together now stand divided in trial or in triumph? Perhaps neither of us knew how closely we felt tied to them until the moment of crisis arrived. It is certain that neither of us realized how deeply we were still rooted in Jewish tradition until we all stood once again, so unexpectedly, before the Western Wall of the Temple in Old Jerusalem. Irony of ironies, it is that archaic religious symbol which, more than anything else, explains to agnostics and to liberals, to secularists and the non-observant, who the people of Israel is.

So in one incredible week we reclaimed two strands of our old Jewish hope. We saw God save our people Israel and we recognized personally how our individual being was tied to our Covenant folk. And now we could feel free to speak of what had sounded so hollow in the post-Holocaust days, that we have from time to time felt his help and presence in our own lives. In the face of our people's disaster, schooled in secular disbelief, how could we say God still works in human lives and that we hope in him? Now what we have seen broadcast before the entire world makes it possible for us to say, in all humility, He has helped us too. Our experience as a community is once again linked with our individual experience and the old pattern of Covenant hope on these two levels reasserts itself.

What we have now regained is not a soothing easy hope. It encompasses of necessity the reality of pain, even of incredible, inexplicable suffering. It does not relish such experiences nor find them a virtue to be cherished. The suffering of the servant has been foisted on us. The crucifixion is not one of our models. Gladly would we await the messiah with the normal tests of endurance. Yet in the midst of whatever bondage history may now bring we can once again hope in God's action on our behalf. He did so for our fathers. He did so in our time. We trust he will do so again for our children and our children's children. His Covenant with us remains unbroken.

We do not understand how to explain in technically coherent terms our strange history of service, of suffering and of continued hope. We know that what we have seen gives us no intellectual clarity about the continuing problems of individual Jews and Jewish communities, of persons and peoples of every faith and none. We still can say nothing about the Holocaust. History is grimmer than we ever imagined and human existence far more difficult than we believed. Still, amidst that realism we have a sense of hope. We know that God may try us, but he does not entirely abandon us. We know our individual existence and social destiny do not escape his saving power. In such a world as ours that is a lot to know. It is the only kind of hope which has a chance to be the answer to despair.

And knowing that much, must not even we secularized Jews follow the organic development of Biblical Judaism and move on from personal and social hope to a full-throated eschatological belief? That surely is incompatible with secularity, but now that we have seen the secular transcended in our own lives we may find the way to reassert in our own accents the coming of his Kingdom which will transform and redeem history. That is more than can be said at present. Indeed already the cynics and the sophisticated are eager to analyze away the religious reality of what we have so freshly gained. I trust that despite their numbers and their stature they will not succeed, but rather that the promise of the unknown prophet of the Exile will be fulfilled:

> *Why sayest thou, O Jacob,*
> *And speakest, O Israel:*
> *"My way is hid from the LORD,*
> *And my right is passed over from my God"?*
> *Hast thou not known? hast thou not heard*
> *That the everlasting God, the LORD,*
> *The Creator of the ends of the earth,*
> *Fainteth not, neither is weary?*
> *His discernment is past searching out.*
> *He giveth power to the faint:*
> *And to him that hath no might He increaseth strength.*
> *Even the youths shall faint and be weary,*
> *And the young men shall utterly fall;*
> *But they that wait for the LORD shall renew their strength;*
> *They shall mount up with wings as eagles;*
> *They shall run, and not be weary;*
> *They shall walk, and not faint.*

(Is. 40, 27-31)*

SUGGESTED READING

Baeck, Leo. *The Essence of Judaism* (New York: Schocken, 1961).
Buber, Martin. *Eclipse of God* (New York: Harper and Row, 1957).
————*The Way of Man* (New York: Citadel Press, 1966).
Schechter, Solomon. *Some Aspects of Rabbinic Theology* (New York: Schocken) n.d.

* The Holy Scriptures (New York: Jewish Publication Society of America, 1917).

MARY A. SCHALDENBRAND

Time, the Self, and Hope: An Intersubjective Interpretation

MARY A. SCHALDENBRAND presents a philosophical essay, "Time, the Self, and Hope: An Intersubjective Interpretation," probing the existential presuppositions for a hopeful future. A student of Paul Ricoeur, Dr. Schaldenbrand brings to an American audience a profound and sensitive understanding of European personalist philosophy and a provocative philosophic starting-point for Christian theologians exploring hope.

A teacher of philosophy at Nazareth College, Kalamazoo, Michigan, she is also a scholar, lecturer, and author. She has done post-doctoral research in philosophical anthropology as a Fulbright scholar at Louvain and research in the philosophy of freedom as proposed by Sartre and by Marcel.

Her published works are essays in *The Primacy of the Person* (Notre Dame: Fides Press, 1967); *Studies in Philosophy and the History of Philosophy* (Washington: Catholic University Press, 1961). Articles which have appeared include "Self-becoming and the Other," *Thought*, 41 (Fall 1966); "Freedom and the I: An Existential Inquiry," *International Philosophical Quarterly* (Winter

1963). She has also contributed essays to *The New Nuns* (New York: The New American Library, 1967) and to *The Changing Sister* (Notre Dame: Fides Press, 1965), both edited by Sister Charles Borromeo Muckenhirn; and to *Twentieth Century Thinkers* (New York: Alba House, 1966).

THE FUTURE as the presence of shared hope—this theme, so rich in harmonies and evocative power, strikes me as less a statement than a summons or, better perhaps, an appeal. For the hopeful future here invoked scarcely goes without saying. On the contrary, its conditions of emergence are extremely arduous. That is why, in seeking to understand this theme, I am led first to explore what I take to be its concrete or existential presuppositions.

But what are these existential presuppositions? It seems to me they are mainly two: namely, time and the self lived intersubjectively. Precisely as lived, however, these two are one. Each includes the other and both always go together in existential unity. In fact, as I will try to show, the future as presence of shared hope requires nothing less than conversion to this new mode of existence.

I use the term "conversion" advisedly. For our life begins, and strongly tends to continue, in alienated time as alienated subjectivity. We begin, as Paul Ricoeur says, "lost among things." To recover ourselves we need deliverance from the alienated ways of living time and self which pervade our initial and accustomed world, the familiar world of spontaneous belief and common sense. Or, in positive terms, we need conversion to an existential mode properly called "intersubjective."

Still, despite their existential unity, I have chosen to consider human time and the personal subject successively rather than simultaneously. For in this way the difference of their bearing on hope is better brought out. Accordingly, my reflections proceed in two movements or phases: a first phase explores the relation between intersubjective time and the future as hopeful presence; a second phase examines the bond between shared hope and the intersubjective self.

Intersubjective Time and the Future as Hopeful Presence

Understanding the time of dialogue, still less living time as dialogue, is clearly not a simple matter. We do well, it seems, to approach the time of dialogue in terms of its opposite: the time of alienation. Against the background of a time which subverts presence, the time which installs presence stands out in sharp relief.

Augustine knew well how to describe this subversive power of a time which alienates.[1] Everyone knows his relentless reduction of the calendar's thick time to the evanescent point of the instant: The year, the month, the week, the day, the hour, the minute, the second—each is divisible into a part which is not yet and a part which no longer is. All that remains as not divisible into future and past is the measureless point of the present, as it were a "something nothing," the no-time of the instant. How find a foothold on the indivisible point between before and after? How hold onto a life whose "nows" slip away even as they come to be? If, as Augustine concludes, time is "the measure of that which is not yet as it passes into that which no longer is by way of that which has no measure," then there seems nothing to do but turn from the world of time where nothing endures and flee to the eternal world where all things changelessly abide.

Today, it is true, few of us incline to follow Augustine in his flight to a timeless world. For, in the interim, we have learned to take a lively interest in this changing world. Theory and practice, evolutionary models and the marvels of technology, encourage us to regard time and change not as signs of lesser being but as ways to more being. With Bergson, we tend to think: Time is creative or it is nothing at all.

Yet this is not to say that we moderns generally live time creatively. On the contrary, it seems all too clear that an evolutionist mentality, enthusiasm in face of rapidly and radically changing times, are by no means proof against alienating modes of time. Most of us in fact find something of ourselves in Heidegger's description of inauthentic temporality.

In describing the time of alienation, Heidegger speaks pointedly to the future as presence. He shows, for example, how a life-style dominated by curiosity perforce comports a temporality devoid of presence. To be sure, the present of the curious self is filled with innumerable objects. Still, none of these objects is allowed to become a presence. For the curious self flits from one to another without resting or pausing. Before any one of them can take shape, acquire consistency, and thus unfold as a presence, the curious self is elsewhere. As Heidegger says: it makes objects present, not to achieve a presence but only to have a present.[2]

And yet, paradoxically, this present which the curious self wants to have is precisely what it wants to escape. That is why, directly on being seen, present objects quickly yield to some future attraction. Nor is the future attraction really a presence. It is rather a phantom of the curious self's desire. Restless desire, not presence, presides over the time of curiosity. Desire drives the self from the "now" to the "new" in a circular and unending escape from the present to the future, from the future to the present.

Because its future and present lack presence, curiosity is a life-style lived as forgetfulness. This forgetfulness can be understood in two ways. In one way, it amounts to an ordinary forgetfulness, the forgetfulness common to superficial people who want only to see and not to understand. In another and deeper sense, however, it means self-forgetfulness. The curious self forgets and forgets itself. Since to forget itself means not to return on its past self, the past of curiosity is likewise devoid of presence.

As comporting self-forgetfulness, the time of curiosity joins other modes of temporal alienation. What unites them is their common opposition to the future as presence. In the existential mode of fear, for example, the self forgets itself as possibility of acting effectively in the world. Powerless, vacillating among possibilities that it cannot make its own, the fearful self awaits the future as a fatality, a not-yet factuality which, on becoming present, threatens to extinguish even the minimal light of its present game of mirrors. Or, again, in the existential mode of inauthentic preoccupation, the self forgets itself as freedom. Here, too, though anticipated with longing rather than dread, the future comes from outside; it advances toward the self as a not-yet eventuality. To be sure, precisely as anticipated, the future is in some way present. Yet it is not properly a presence, for the free and effective self which presence presupposes is absent.

Why presence presupposes a free and effective self will appear clearly only at the end of these reflections on intersubjective time. At this point, however, it is already possible to observe how inauthentic existence takes the self to be fundamentally passive toward time. According to it, the self is in time as the prey of time. Time measures out its existence drop by drop. The future is seen as holding in reserve an unknown number of "nows"; these emerge singly from behind the curtain of the "not yet" and file across the stage of the present only to lose themselves in the "no longer is" of an irretrievable past. Here Augustine and Heidegger seem to meet.

And yet they are worlds apart. For Heidegger the self is not merely "in time" or temporal. Rightly understood, the self is in itself temporalizing. To exist as an authentic self is less to suffer time as a fate than to effect time as a work. If we wish to understand the future as presence, it seems to me that we must penetrate the sense of this Heideggerian reversal.[3]

Contrast may serve to sharpen the difference between being in time and making time be. For the temporalizing self of authentic existence, the future is not simply a fact which, while "not yet," will be "soon." Rather, its future is an act, a projecting that ties in together with itself the "not yet" and the "soon." Neither is the past of this temporalizing self a fact which, having been "before," is "no longer." On the contrary, as continuing return on itself, its past is a continuous retrieve of itself as "having been." Finally, the present of a time-creative self could hardly consist in a series of colorless "nows." Precisely because this self makes itself present to its "nows," its "now" is unique and significant.

As act, not fact, the time of authentic existence overcomes alienation in two ways especially: First, it integrates the three temporal dimensions. For this act anticipates the future, retrieves the past, and attends to the present in a single, though diversified, movement. Thereby it overcomes the dispersion, the power of fragmentation, which lurks in the "not yet," the "having been," and the "now." Secondly, because the three temporal dimensions are also and equally dimensions of the self, their integration is equivalent to self-integration. To unify them is to restore the integral self of future, past, and present. When the self as possibility, history, and actuality is thus unified, its power of presence is immeasurably heightened.

Only this integral self, it seems right to suppose, can live the future as presence. For surely the "presence" in question is not the dubious or minimal "present" of curiosity or fear or inauthentic preoccupation. Indeed, thanks to Heidegger's analysis of authentic temporality, the future as presence is greatly clarified. Not only does it presuppose the full-bodied presence of the integral self: as integrating the three temporal dimensions, its futurity is "thick" with past and present.

According to Heidegger, there is one future whose presence so integrates time or the self that it frees passage from inauthentic to authentic existence. This future is nothing other than every self's ownmost possibility: namely, the possibility of its impossibility or, more simply, its death. When, in anguish, the self anticipates its extreme possibility, it returns by that very movement on its radical origin as "always already" a "fallen" freedom, a finite freedom "thrown" into the world; then, given the self's resolute acceptance of itself as finite freedom destined-to-death, this same movement restores the self to its present. Now, however, the present no longer appears to it as mere mélange or flux of circumstances but as truly its own situation; that is, a synthesis of what is imposed on it and what is willed by it. To live its situation in truth is the privilege of the integral self, the self of integral time, whose regard is fixed inflexibly on its being-unto-death.

Not that the presence of its future death converts the self to authentic existence "once and for all." Heidegger insists on this: conversion to authentic existence is a continuing conquest which, never finished and ever menaced, remains always precarious. For, as the self's extreme possibility, death is far from being merely the actual moment which ends its life. Rather, it is the ever-present possibility which the self "has to be." Thereby death is taken up into life. The self is dying, "facing death," as long as it lives. That, too, is why the resolve of authentic existence never pays "once and for all" its debt to anguish. Resolutely to accept itself as radical finitude is inevitably to face itself with an anguish that cannot be surmounted but only assumed.

Heidegger's analysis of death as the future presence which permits passage to authentic existence is at first sight convincing. Nothing so delivers the self from illusions, it would appear, as the regard which sees all things, the self included, *sub specie mortis*. And yet second thoughts are irrepressible. It seems to me that we must ask Heidegger: Is not the anguish which leads only to acceptance of radical finitude a blind alley? Is not radical finitude the very thing that we can never accept? Is not hope the refusal of this acceptance?

Why Heidegger's "being-unto-death" fails as a future presence derives mainly from this: It nowhere opens onto hope. Not that Heidegger takes death too seriously. Hardly anything is more damaging to hope than repressing or camouflaging the reality of death. The problem is rather that he does not take death seriously enough. For his interpretation misses what gives death its utmost seriousness, namely, its intersubjective sense.[4]

This criticism may appear unfair. After all, Heidegger elsewhere clearly affirms that being-with-others fundamentally characterizes human reality. Besides, the resolve of authentic temporality seems to include a reference to others and true being-in-common. For, in presence of its being-unto-death, is not the self freed from a false self-importance? Does it not thereby become able to regard others with that radical tolerance which, in Heidegger's profound sense, "lets their being be"?

It is true, of course, that Heidegger describes human being as essentially "with-others." Yet it is also true that analysis of intersubjectivity, that is, the co-presence of subjects precisely *as* subjects, is notably missing in his work.[5] In any case, the authentic temporality of conversion to authentic existence proceeds without reference to co-presence. That is why the resolve of authentic temporality could conceivably work against true being-in-common. It is possible that, in presence of my being-unto-death, I would lose not only a false sense of importance but all sense of any importance; in that event, I would become indifferent to everyone, myself and others. Or, worse still, my resolve to accept radical finitude could lead, not to radical tolerance of others but to radical contempt for others since, in the end like myself, they must die anyway.

Still, the question implied in the foregoing objection demands an answer: Why is a hopeful future presence required to be intersubjective? To pretend to answer this question in a definitive or fully conclusive way would be presumptuous. And yet there are persuasive indications of an indissoluble bond between the co-presence of subjects and the presence of a hopeful future. Three indications in particular strike me as highly significant: (1) the integration of self-time occurs in the "with" of co-presence; reversely, alienated self-time attends the breakdown of the capacity for co-presence; (2) the experience of creative duration occurs especially in the dialogic relation of love or friendship; contrariwise, the sterile time of fixation or repetition attends the incapacity of dialogue; (3) the self's ease in duration, its confidence and suppleness therein, is not unrelated to the quality of its communication with itself; in turn, the quality of its communication with itself corresponds to the quality of its communication with others.

Experience shows how the "with" of intersubjective communion integrates self-time. An especially instructive example, perhaps, is the privileged "with" of sexual union. When sexual union is what it signifies, that is, the self-donation of each partner to the other, it engenders a future. To the hopeful presence of this future, this history which they will make together, the partners bring all their living past. Whatever has shaped them or impressed them, whatever has entered into their present selves, is here brought into play, not as dead, but in vital communion with the hopeful presence of their intimacy.

The experience of friendship confirms in its own way the integrating effect of the "with." In presence of one whose affectionate regard is deep and abiding, the self awakens to its possibilities and, to this awakening, brings all the living resources of its past. Why the self finds friendship so livening hereby becomes plain: through friendship the self rises to a hopeful future and recuperates its past, all in the heightened awareness of its present "presence."

More grimly instructive, however, is the case of alienated self-time. Psychotherapy, in particular contemporary dialogic therapy, makes painfully clear the tie between alienated temporality and the breakdown of co-presence. Describing the alienated time of certain patients, Dr. Lévy-Valensi writes: "Time is frozen or disconnected. Memory ceases to be 'personal,' the past is objectified into biography. Then, to speak as Kierkegaard, "The 'I' is deadened to such a point that it lives in the third person."[6] Of special interest here is the dual requirement for recovering "first-person" time: If the patient is to rediscover integrated time, he must recover himself; but, if he is to recover himself, the patient must rediscover relation to the other. To be sure, Freud was already well aware of this, for he knew the importance of transference in the psychoanalytic cure. Yet today's therapists, by stressing above all the doctor-patient relationship, unequivocally affirm the close bond between integrated self-time and co-presence.

For the self of integrated time, duration is experienced as creative. To live in it is to participate in an adventure felt to be moving forward. It is to live with the expectation that time can bring something new, some "good news."

With good reason, Gabriel Marcel links this creative duration with intersubjective encounter.[7] For, as freedom, the personal subject is source of innovation, of new truth and being. When personal subjects live the appeal-response dialectic within the freedom-promotive milieu of friendship, time becomes the carrier of invention and development.

In sharp contrast to creative duration is the sterile time of fixation or repetition, the no-time of illusion and immobility. Few places are as depressing to visit as the asylum ward: the hebephrenic patient with neither future nor past nor present, the manic-depressive awaiting the future not as time of accomplishment but as catastrophic end, the obsessive neurotic blindly and compulsively repeating the past—all these attest that time, as soon as it ceases to be invention, becomes for the one who lives it the measure of his illness, the prison of his pain. Again, however, what is especially to the point here is the dual conclusion of therapists: the inability to live time creatively corresponds to an incapacity for communication; to restore the patient to creative duration is to restore him to communication.[8]

But restoring the patient to creative duration is clearly no simple matter. Living time inventively supposes the very thing the patient cannot manage: namely, an ease, a suppleness, a way of relaxing in duration. Marcel rightly notes a "secret affinity" between this relaxation and hope.[9] To hope is surely to refuse a closed time, a time that brings nothing new. Still, nonacceptance of closed time occurs, not through stiffening in resolve, but by "relaxing in presence of. . . ." Only the self that knows how to yield itself, to confide itself in duration as the swimmer confides himself to the sea, is able to discover creative duration, the hopeful presence of the future.

To ask the self to confide itself, however, is already to acknowledge that, in itself, the self is intersubjective. That is, the self is a presence not only to others but also to itself. How this dual self-presence relates to shared hope is the question that guides the second phase of these reflections.

The Intersubjective Self and Shared Hope

Today it is well said: Human being is such that, for it, its being is in question. Or, as some prefer: The being of human being is to be concerned about its being. Self-concern thus belongs essentially to the self. But, for hope, everything depends on *how* the self concerns itself.

There are ways of being self-concerned that ruin the

chances of hope. Examples are not hard to find. The self may be to itself as an anxious owner to a threatened possession; then it stiffens itself and asserts itself defensively. Or the self may concentrate on itself as a hypochondriac concentrates on health; in this case, it becomes like Marcel's man with an abscessed tooth who must experiment cautiously with hot and cold and who, in general, resembles a moving and highly vulnerable enclosure. Still again, the self may treat itself as a manager treats a star performer; here the emphasis is on performance and "getting to the top." What is common to these modes of self-concern is their opposition to the conditions that give hope its chance: namely, the "with" proper to subjects and the self's relaxed ease.

In marked contrast to the self-concern that subverts hope, there is a self-concern that opens onto hope. To understand it Marcel proposes an analogy which, though obviously inadequate, may yet prove helpful. Within the situation of test or trial, the situation that hope always supposes, the self is "with" and "to" itself as an older brother is "with" and "to" a younger brother.[10] Through Marcel's analogy, three aspects of hopeful self-concern come to light: first, the self's concern for itself is here the concern of friendship, that is, concern for its being as subject; second, this concern is supportive, for herein the self assures itself that, in the end and thanks to its trial, it will become the self it would be but is not yet; third, as if in presence of its promised being, the self holds itself within its test situation, not rigidly, but with the ease and "give" of a patience properly called "creative."

This creative patience of the self with itself, however, is best understood through reflection on patience with others.[11] Well understood, patience with others means not a simple indifference to others which, under pretext of "accepting" them, merely abandons them to themselves. To be sure, patience refuses to do violence to others by imposing upon them a temporal rhythm not their own. But, in addition, creative patience embraces with trust their temporal rhythms. In communicating to others its confidence, it conspires with their rhythms from within and thus tends to exercise upon them a transforming influence. This is the reason of its creativity.

To illustrate its creativity, Marcel cites the example of a flustered student at his oral examination. If the examiner is creatively patient, he will say: "Take your time," and his meaning will be: "Do not force the personal rhythm, the proper cadence of your reflection, or even of your memory, for if you do you will spoil your chances, you will be likely to say at random the first words which come into your head." On hearing these words, on feeling the respectful confidence of the co-presence they express, the flurried candidate is enabled to "take his time" and, thereby, to be creatively patient with himself.

But it would be a mistake to take the detour of "patience with others" for a pedagogic device only. As the above illustration shows, patience with ourselves is in fact mediated by the patience of others. Or, in other words, the self-concern that gives hope its chance is first learned from others, received through others. Of course, to point this out is to say nothing new. Hegel made the same point some years ago when he said: The self is a mediated reality.

Still, though not news, the mediated character of the self's presence to itself is highly important for hope. In metaphoric language, Marcel indicates the reason.[12] He says in effect: If I form with myself a community, this community is by no means a monad. It cannot establish itself as a distinct and isolated center without working for its own destruction. On the contrary, it draws the elements of its life from what is brought to it along canals from other friendly communities, communities whose names and situations, however, it often hardly knows. It is to a consciousness of these reciprocities, of this mysterious and incessant circulation, that I open myself when I hope.

Through this opening, the relation between shared hope and the intersubjective self begins to appear. If the self forms with itself a community, a "we," and if, as "we," it hopes for itself, then it surely follows: the subject of hope is not "I" but "we." But if, in addition, the "we" of the self-community is the tributary of all other communities so that its life is from and with them, then there is no denying: Hope is nothing if it is not shared.

To be sure, the "we" of hope in this dual and far-reaching sense is not "given" but only intended. Or, better perhaps, the subject of hope is itself hoped for. But, insofar as the self opens itself to awareness of "this mysterious and incessant circulation" between the "we" of the self-community and the "we" of all other friendly communities, it becomes more truly the subject of hope.

For the subject of hope, then, giving hope its chance means participating ever more fully in the human community. In three ways especially, this participation offers to hope something like a foothold:

First of all, insofar as participants seek to humanize a situation—whether by science, art, social action or whatever—they anticipate a hopeful future. To participate seriously in a project is at least to wager that "some good will come of it."

Secondly, insofar as participants manage to overcome obstacles and to make progress, however modest, in humanizing a situation, they say in effect: Reality, after all, is not ultimately hostile or cruelly indifferent to human purposes and hopes.

Thirdly, insofar as participants create a community of friendship, they engage in recognition-events. Within these events, each self becomes aware of itself as deserving respect through becoming aware of another's respectful awareness. Thanks to their mutual acts of affirmative recognition, they increasingly understand themselves as free, unique, and endless possibility of intersubjective communication.

But, though living the self intersubjectively gives hope a chance, it cannot claim to do more than that. I have advisedly used formulas like "offering hope a foothold" and "giving hope its chance." What I wish to emphasize thereby is that hope is never "guaranteed" in advance. Hope does not "follow logically" as a conclusion follows from premises, nor does it "follow naturally" as day follows night. Above all, hope is never the prize of technique.

And yet the importance of giving hope its opportunity can scarcely be exaggerated. Today more than ever, perhaps, there is reason to insist on this point. In face of a cheery optimism, a bland confidence in technology and evolution, "timid hope" is obliged to retreat. In fact, it is banished before it appears on the scene. What place can there be for hope in a world where everything is bound to "turn out for the best"? What need is there for hope when all that is really needed is know-how, firm determination and, above all, "positive thinking"? To appear at all, hope requires a situation where the reality of evil is felt so profoundly that despair becomes fully possible. For, when it deserves its name, hope exists as traversing the menace of despair.

Paradoxical as it may seem, the reality of evil is experienced with greater severity as life is lived more intersubjectively. This can be seen by observing what happens when evil invades the "with" of friendship. Consider, for example, the evil of death, political and social evils, the evil that murders the innocent and destroys even the just:

(1) Death acquires its full weight only in the context of presence. Understood in terms of the self alone, death could conceivably be acceptable as a final "falling off to sleep." But, understood as the destruction of intimate co-presence, death can never be acceptable. The lover cannot resolve to accept the destruction of presence. To love another in depth is to say, You whom I love, you will never die. Precisely by appearing to be the "end of presence," death invites despair. If this despair is to be overcome, it is only by hoping "in spite of" all the appearances.

(2) In the same way, the crushing weight of political and social evils is felt only within the human community. In fact, the degree of involvement in building up this community is the measure of anguish in face of atrocities committed against it. The gas chambers of Auschwitz, the fires of Hiroshima and Nagasaki, "search and destroy" operations in the villages of Vietnam, rat-infested tenements in Harlem and Watts—these tempt to despair especially those whose lives are "for" and "with" the human community.

(3) But it is above all the death of the innocent child and the suffering of the just that tempt to despair those whose care is the human community. Out of the depths of his concern, Camus could ask: Is human existence itself *The Plague*? And Job, type of the suffering just, raises the ultimate spectre for lovers of justice: Is it possible that God himself is the evil one?

Not only, then, does life lived intersubjectively give hope its chance by intensifying the affirmative experience of co-presence. It also gives hope its chance by intensifying the negative experience of destruction and death. Only to the superficial will this paradoxical situation seem odd.

NOTES

[1] *The Confessions of St. Augustine,* trans. Edward B. Pusey (New York: Random House, Modern Library edition, 1949), Bk. XI.

[2] *Being and Time,* trans. John Macquarrie and Edward Robinson (New York: Harper & Brothers, 1962), p. 397. For this discussion of inauthentic temporality, I have relied especially on the section: "Temporality and Everydayness," pp. 385-401.

[3] *Ibid.,* pp. 374-80.

[4] I realize that, in Heidegger's later writings, authentic existence is reinterpreted in terms of the relation of Being to man. Authentic existence thereby comes to mean an existence in which man fulfills his essence by answering the "call" of Being. However, since this Being is "wholly other" than man and its "call" is silent, it seems to me that the later authenticity is as void of intersubjectivity as is that of *Being and Time.*

[5] In particular, as Heidegger himself admits, this co-presence is "undone" when the human existent faces death as its ownmost possibility: "When it stands before itself in this way, all its relations to any other Dasein have been undone. This ownmost *non-relational* possibility is at the same time the uttermost one." (Italics mine.)

[6] *Le dialogue psychanalytique* (Paris: Presses Universitaires de France, 1962), p. 191.

[7] *Creative Fidelity,* trans. Robert Rosthal (New York: The Noonday Press, 1965), p. 12.

[8] Lévy-Valensi, *op. cit.,* pp. 189-98.

[9] *Homo Viator,* trans. Emma Craufurd (New York: Harper Torchbooks, 1963), pp. 38-9.

[10] *Creative Fidelity,* p. 42.

[11] *Ibid.,* pp. 39-40.

[12] *Ibid.,* p. 61.

SUGGESTED READING

Heidegger, Martin. *Being and Time* (New York: Harper and Row, 1962).
Lévy-Valensi, Eliane. *Le dialogue psychanalytique.*
Marcel, Gabriel. *Creative Fidelity* (New York: Farrar Straus, 1964). *Homo Viator* (Magnolia, Mass.: Peter Smith) n.d.

DAVID BURRELL, C.S.C.

Faith and the Nature
of the Mind as Inquiry

REV. DAVID BURRELL, a member of the Congregation of the Holy Cross, who teaches philosophy at the University of Notre Dame, is one of a core of talented young American scholars within the Catholic tradition. "Faith and the Nature of the Mind as Inquiry" is a philosophical inquiry into the ground of Truth underlying faith which makes hope possible. While acknowledging his debt to Bernard Lonergan, S.J., Father Burrell is himself a specialist in the logic of metaphysical and theological discourse. His teaching career began in 1964 with his appointment at the University of Notre Dame following completion of studies at the Gregorian University, Rome; at Laval University, Quebec; and at Yale University, from which he received his doctorate. He has been the recipient of Fulbright, Woodrow Wilson, and Kent fellowships.

Father Burrell is the editor of Father Bernard Lonergan's *Verbum: Word and Ideas in Aquinas* (Notre Dame: Notre Dame University Press, 1967). His own publications include: "C. S. Peirce: Pragmaticism as a Theology of Judgment," *International Philosophical Quarterly*, 5 (December 1965); "God: Language and Transcendence," *The Commonweal*, 85 (February 10, 1967); and numerous other articles for religious journals.

I WOULD LIKE to explore the possible ways we might speak of one's faith as genuine or true. I have chosen to position this investigation within the broader and more natural scope of *inquiry* because this context seems to me a more appropriate one for discussing the thorny topic of truth. I shall not concern myself directly with stereotyped "theories of truth," but rather sketch out some paradigm ways in which we use the term *true* and ask whether any of these ways can shed light on the human-divine enterprise of faith. My general indebtedness to Bernard Lonergan will appear throughout. I mention this only to help orient the reader, not to cover over the ineptitudes that are bound to mar an endeavor as searching as this one.

There is a good deal of dissatisfaction among Catholic theologians about scholastic theories of truth and their suitability when speaking of the assent of faith. It would be tempting to confront this malaise with a careful development of a classical position like that of Aquinas. The result would in many cases expose the dissatisfaction as misunderstanding. But this would do little more than prolong a polemic already too abstract and wearisome. So with the initial admission of guidance by Lonergan, I shall eschew an explicit treatment of theories of truth, and try to approach more closely to our shared experience of faith and inquiry by some careful attention to usage and a generous sampling of examples.

First, a distinction often overlooked in our haste to speak of *truth:* the distinction between meaning and truth, between understanding what has been said and assessing its correctness. Eager students are normally anxious to find out whether what a book or teacher says is really true. Part of a teacher's task is to rein them in, to remind them that learning is first a matter of finding out what is meant. Assuming that something can be taught, what is taught is what an author meant, not whether or not he is in fact on target. What can be taught is a point of view or a theory, not whether what it presents is actually the case.

Although this distinction between understanding and judgment is thoroughly classical, it has a way of breaking in as news on a philosophical school or an individual student. Part of the fault lies with our native attraction to a crude psychology which links words directly with things. There seems to be a fear, sometimes worked up into philosophical theses, that once such a linkage is loosened, we are in danger of losing our native realistic contact with the world. But it is not realism so much as nativism which is in jeopardy. For the smallest bit of reflection assures us that words do not point, but they can make sense. Whatever relation there is between word and world is forged by the rules relating word with word into a language. Words derive whatever sense they have from their uses within the language of which they are a part, and those which do refer to something do so via their established sense.

Now "sense" is offered here as a synonym for "meaning," but we count on "sense" for other duties as well. When a proposal "makes sense" it is thereby acclaimed as *right*; "sense" connotes direction, and so suggests the act of pointing, and what "makes sense" is on target. So the distinction between meaning and truth is just that, a distinction. The two do not form watertight compartments. There is a pregnant sense of understanding a presentation which presses for agreement or disagreement. Notice that the assessment is already implicit when we speak of understanding a *situation* rather than a presentation. To understand a situation *is* to grasp what indeed is the case. If one's account is challenged, the challenge amounts to saying that the account does not faithfully represent the state of affairs it pretends to present. The form of the challenge is normally: "But you don't seem to *understand* so-and-so's position in all this, etc." That is to say, the reporter has misconstrued the *situation*. Things are in fact different from what his account makes them out to be. So understanding strains towards judgment just as language purports to articulate an actual state of affairs, the "lay" of an institution, or one's feelings at the moment.

The observation that words are not to be construed as linked directly with things helped to throw into relief the distinction between meaning and truth. Yet, once having clarified this point, we must move beyond it. For words do of course refer to things, or more accurately and more classically, statements normally refer, and for the most part intend to refer, to states of affairs or situations. So we can say that a statement is a true statement when it is on target, when it faithfully describes the situation it purports to describe. But words and sentences can have meaning without referring to anything. At least we must be able to discern their meaning prior to and independent of their supposed referent. Meaning and truth, then, remain distinct issues, no matter how organically related they may be to one another in actual inquiry.

The distinction between meaning and truth harbors the fact that understanding and judgment represent qualitatively distinct activities. When oriented to action, they are reflected in deliberation and judgment. Understanding and deliberation are concerned with what can be communicated and shared; judgment and decision engage what is unique and separate in each of us. This simply recalls what I have insisted on so far, namely that meaning has to do with whatever can be taught, communicated and shared, while truth can be claimed only subsequent to appraisal or judgment.

In a Personal Sense

But where meaning is both shared and personal, where "meaning" suggests "a direction for my life," then a project or a proposal cannot claim to give meaning to my life unless it also *claims* to be true. Although a proposed way of life can "make sense" without my having to face up to whether or not it is true, I cannot take it up as something which *gives* sense or meaning to my life unless I am prepared to accept it as true. So in this personal and existential situation, meaning and truth seem to converge.

Now the sense of "true" has most certainly shifted when I speak of a proposed way of life being *true*. "True" no longer means a faithful description or claims that a statement is somehow "on target." It is closer to "true-for-me," but implies something more. A projected way of life might be acclaimed *true* if it proved to be "faithful to the inner laws of human growth and development." But expressions like these are highly metaphorical. Would anyone care to lay out the "laws of human development"? We assume there are such largely because it is inconceivable that an orderly result may be obtained in an utterly random fashion. Yet any attempt to spell them out simply exposes the original metaphor of *laws* by having recourse to more openly evocative usage—like openness and fruitfulness. To try to pin them down any more than this, to think of human development and achievement as literally codified into laws, is a temptation which leads to metaphysics of an uncritical sort. But without some touchstone, it looks as though existential truth collapses into "what gives meaning to (my) life." For we have already noted how we demand that a proposal be true if it promises to contribute to my development. And if there be no other way to assess its truth other than its effect on my development, then the two are identical. This is not the end of the road, of course, for there are certainly ways of discriminating genuine growth from the spurious and rank. But to recognize these shifts does effectively relocate the question of truth and meaning in those realizations that are deeply personal.

It might be helpful to retrace the path of our relocation. To hunt for a touchstone or try to carve out a set of laws for genuine human development is a temptation because judging that a proposed life-style is *true* when it contributes to "genuine or authentic selfhood" is a quite different procedure from counting a statement true when it succeeds in adequately describing a situation. The procedures are different because proposals and exhortations differ from simple statements, and what makes statements simple is that their truth can be checked: "There are seven bottles left in the refrigerator. There are not. Go see for yourself." And further still, a proposal that pretends to give meaning to one's life is at once more intimate, more demanding and yet more vague than a proposal to execute certain maneuvers at half-time. A drill team has clear standards to meet and can meet them. But the price of well-defined success seems to be artificiality and removed from the rich give-and-take of life. But are we to say that there are no standards, no touchstones, no means of verifying a proposed life-project? Since standards and criteria are not the sort of things that one finds or not, to argue for their presence or absence is really to query the appropriateness of a certain way of thinking and speaking about life-projects and proposals that mean to give meaning to persons' lives. If we are to speak of *truth* in the area of faith and life-project, then

we must come to terms with standards, criteria and the like.
But we have already seen how the issues surrounding claims
and assessments of truth shift when we are dealing with personal and existential issues. Presumably the standards, the
touchstones, and the methods of verification will function
differently as well. The question then remains: how useful will
it be to continue to speak of *truth* when the horizons are so
different? My contention is that it will prove useful, and the
argument runs as follows: If we follow our instinct to speak of
a proposed way of life as true, the attempt to assimilate cog-
nate notions like standard, criteria, and verification will actually feed back on the more accepted uses of these terms in a
way that illuminates some hitherto unexplored aspects of the
more accepted usage.

Truth and Fidelity

Divergent religious postures since the sixteenth century in the
West have certainly not made this effort any easier. In fact,
issues surrounding faith and the assent of faith have been so
neatly and effectively polarized that it is difficult to raise the
question of truth without being forced into one or another
position. The Catholic school has proved in general to be con-
ceptualist in persuasion. Although faith was always acknowledged to be "something more" than assent to a set of propositions, the propositional assent was just as universally regarded
as the controlling axis of the action. Propositional assent lends
itself to questions of truth or falsity, so it has never seemed
inappropriate to raise this question in a Catholic context. But
how the truth claimed for the statements linked up with one's
religious life remained in obscurity. And the reason for this

should be clear to us now. Insistence on the truth of statements leads one to expect descriptions and to verify them in familiar ways. It offers little hint of the unique properties of a truth which is assessed in intimate relation to one's life and its need for direction. In short, the special character of "religious truth" is glossed over, the inherent connection between theological reflection and interior life overlooked, and our native tendency to literalism granted abundant support.

The more common Protestant tendency, of course, formed the polar opposite of the Catholic, and religious differences tended to reinforce the opposition. Here the accent lay heavily on the "something more," on the commitment whereby one's life was taken up, given over and given sense and direction. No one could ascertain the truth of the direction bestowed prior to living the life itself. With this we shall in part concur, but the weakness of the classical presentation lay in its hesitancy to speak of truth at all. Questions of truth or falsity seemed to imply a preoccupation with statements and what they intend to describe, and since there was nothing specifically religious here, these questions were simply laid aside. The result, of course, was a position on religious questions and discourse peculiarly accommodating to a naturalist reduction procedure and a positivist denial of any cognitive basis for religious faith. Yet the fact is that we do come to know something about the world and about ourselves along the way of religious questing. This must somehow be explained, and with it the role that true/false plays in all this.

Kierkegaard actually represents a mediating element and a bridge to our present thesis. His lapidary statement sounds classically Protestant with its accent on commitment and seeming disregard for content: "an objective uncertainty held fast

in an appropriation process of the most passionate inwardness
is the truth, the highest truth attainable for an existing individual. . . . The truth is precisely the venture which chooses an
objective uncertainty with the passion of the infinite."[1] He is
speaking of the truth of those proposals which purport to give
meaning to one's life. This is clear from the context and from
his explicit avowal: "the above definition of truth is an equivalent expression for faith." Much discussion has raged about
this point, yet for our purposes the statement is straightforward. The accent is clearly on *inwardness,* passionate inwardness. If anything is to be "held fast," it is to be held fast in a
process of appropriation of the most passionate inwardness.
This characterizes Kierkegaard's own life, and the process is
worked out in a style not unlike Plato's *Dialogues,* one which
engages the reader to undergo what is being dramatized so that
he will experience the point. Therefore, the formulation must
be interpreted in the light of Kierkegaard's life and writings,
both of which intertwine to embody and lead us into that passionate inwardness. It is the *within* of this inwardness that
affords the conditions under which the appropriation-process
becomes a kind of verification process. Such at least will be my
thesis.

But the appropriation-verification is dominated by a "holding fast," or I should say *is* itself a holding fast. This insistence
assures us of Kierkegaard's sense for inwardness. For it means
that the appropriation-process cannot be construed as a progressive verification-through-accommodation of popular pragmatism. The sense seems to be that appropriation is achieved
in the measure, and only in the measure, that one realizes his
own identity as well. We shall see how this same point is an
underlying and usually unattended theme of pragmatism. The

most direct guide to our understanding this inward appropria-tion-verification process, however, seems to be Gabriel Marcel and his suggestion that truth in these matters betokens a kind of *fidelity*.

By aligning myself with Marcel I implicitly acknowledge agreement with his thesis of truth as fidelity. But the nature of Marcel's work sets limits on one's agreement with him. I feel that he is on the right track, but that is the most one can say, because his thesis is not so much a thesis as a suggestion. For we have so ask: fidelity to what? to whom? But we have to ask these questions in the spirit in which Marcel offers his sugges-tion. Marcel relies always on the metaphorical and evocative power of the words he chooses to be key terms. (The strength of this approach, its apparent concreteness, can also work against itself. For the resonances are concentrated in key terms nonetheless, and these can easily freeze into a new abstraction, a contemporary jargon, given the tendency of words to come to stand on their own.) The very choice of "fidelity," with its biblical as well as marital connotations, suggests that his use is deliberately tensive. We are constantly being pointed or pulled into an interpersonal situation. "Fidelity" connotes accepting another and being accepted by another. It includes an appar-ent narrowing of perspectives to concretion within a discipline, yet a narrowing which can result in an opening out within oneself and to others. The *other* calls forth the process and is intimately involved in it; fidelity is fidelity to *someone*. The result is not a merger, however, but me: me discovered, me possessed and constituted by the values embodied in the re-solve to remain faithful.

Yet this new me cannot be described simply as someone who has "learned something" and has verified that it is true.

We may indeed *try* to put it that way: "I have learned (for example) that loving is accepting another and the self that this other returns to me. I have learned that to accept in this way is to joy." No one who has grown in fidelity would say that he has *not* learned all this, but the language of "learning something," "learning that such is the case," is derivative and inadequate. What has happened is not primarily a lesson learned but something else that resulted in knowledge of this sort. The key here is the response to the question, "How do you know all this?" "How do I know it? I just know it, that's all!" Or, "When I followed this course of action, these things happened to me, these realizations broke in upon me."

In short, the warrants for the statements made are from within, not from without. The ground is something that has taken place within me and results in an entirely new focus for my activity; it does not lie in some state of affairs. Consider the statements offered, and imagine oneself enunciating them at different times, say a year apart. In the intervening period we can suppose one has lived more or less faithfully within the dimensions projected by the statements. At the year's end, however, we would probably be at a loss to find expression more adequate to the experience than these original statements. So it is with the language of self-realization. But this does not mean they are the same statements. Rather the likelihood is that we would realize their aptness and truth so much more intensely the second time around that we would have to wonder whether we had really understood anything at all when we first enunciated them.

This experience of felt disparity dramatizes the fact that what we have learned can normally be expressed in a proposition and hence assessed in the customary manner, whereas what we have become cannot be expressed or can be so only in a blatantly inadequate way. Aristotle taught us to regard growth as genuine when it proved consonant with man's nature, but what of the individual? Kierkegaard speaks of the self in normative terms implying self-realization: "the condition of the self when despair is completely eradicated: by relating itself to its own self and by willing to be itself, the self is grounded transparently in the Power which posited it."[2] Where Aristotle glossed over the individual, comparing personal development to that of a member of any species, Kierkegaard seems to overlook what we share in common, simply failing to inquire whether there can be any pattern (however flexible) by which the self may be said to relate itself to its own self.

Yet Kierkegaard's seems to be less an oversight than an insight into the limitations of language, of what can be *said*. If there be a pattern, and he thinks there is, it cannot be described with any respectable accuracy (what might it mean to be consonant with one's nature?) but can only be shown or dramatized. The sign that personal growth is genuine seems akin to the fruits of fidelity: a sense of liberation and of peace. One could have recourse to spatial metaphors: a sense of spaciousness, openness, which suggests affinities with the fruitfulness which recommends a scientific hypothesis. All this sounds similar to Dewey's composite description of an inquiry consummated: a release from tension. This has been variously ridiculed, but he has a gloss in more positive terms which comes closer to our point. We have "a first-rate test of the value of any philosophy which is offered us: does it end in conclusions which, when they are referred back to ordinary life-experiences and their predicaments, render them more significant, more luminous to us, and make our dealings with them more fruitful?"[3]

One might presume to measure a "release from tension," but to speak of making experience more significant, more luminous, and our dealings with it more fruitful clearly removes us from the neurological sphere. His recourse to metaphor is of course flagrant, but this too is illustrative. It is illustrative, I take it, of a ground-situation which will admit of no direct expression, no independent set of criteria, but must settle for comparison. And of course it indicates a need to move somewhere beyond the calculable world of stimulus-response. The move, I shall suggest, is *within*.

To recapitulate, Marcel's comparison of truth to fidelity led us to link "true" with "faithful." Since we speak of persons being faithful one to another and associate this with their individual development, we were led to examine what sort of criteria people use for gauging genuine or harmonious development. The criteria I suggested were of course ineluctably vague: a sense of liberation and peace, of inner space. Yet they were surprisingly akin to those suggested by Dewey for evaluating what we can only speak of as a philosophy. All this by way of showing that one can responsibly speak of a projected way of life as true because we can at least broadly describe something like a process of verification. But of course a process whose result is broadly and metaphorically described cannot be called a stepwise procedure, and so is *not* a verification-process in any strict sense at all. Hence the analogy between proposals and propositions, the ordinary sorts of things one can call true or false, is hopelessly strained, so why bother?

The criteria Dewey suggested, however, can be put to our own inquiry. Is it useful to draw a comparison, no matter how far-fetched? Why not simply note how natural it is to refer to personal growth as genuine or authentic, and leave it at that? Why get into questions of the truth or falsity of the ways proposed? Does it prove liberating, luminous with respect to our experience, fruitful in making that experience our own if we assimilate evaluating life patterns to evaluating statements? Is there anything appropriate and hence potentially *true* about the analogy despite all the dissimilarities?

I suggest that there is something appropriate in speaking of personal styles of life and patterns of development as true. Not however because the senses of "true" ordinarily linked with statements can cast much light on the use of "genuine" to assess human growth. But rather because the reflections we have entertained on the inner criteria for genuine development help focus us on the role that judgment plays in assessing propositions. Because "true" can be used of statements, we are tempted to think of it as a possible property they might possess, just as sentences can be long, involved, exclamatory and the rest. But properties are established by observation or by some kind of comparison, whereas truth, we are told, requires an activity quite distinct: an assessment.

There is general agreement here. Assessing is not like comparing. That's the misleading feature of the so-called "correspondence theory of truth." It seems to involve some kind of comparison between statement and world, like a yardstick measuring a surface. And this requires an independent, extra-linguistic access to the world which simply does not square with the recognizably linguistic character of our experience. In what, then, does assessment consist? We must rule out comparison with a standard, since we must speak of the standards or criteria for truth in terms that are inherently vague. This forbids any activity as straightforward as *comparison,* for if the standard is something like "rendering our experience more luminous," how can we compare a statement with that? Charles Peirce speaks of a truth-assessment as springing from or reflecting an "intellectual sympathy"[4] for the statement or thesis proposed, a kind of intellectual feeling of congruence. It is here that pragmatism becomes tender-minded, as we also noted in Dewey. I suspect that we accept those statements as true which open our horizons, give a certain body to our experience, and quite simply enhance our ability to live more fully. This certainly entails a measure of coherence with other propositions that we have already accepted on these or similar grounds, but a coherence which is generally subordinate to a desire to live more integrally and more in communion with the world and with ourselves.

This way of describing the grounds of our acceptance is more evocative than descriptive, and hence irreducibly vague. But not irresponsibly so: It represents an attempt to put into words what we have already avowed that words are inadequate to describe, a process of personal growth or becoming. Fortunately we can rest with the vagueness here, and consider established our simple point: when knowledge moves beyond amassing information, whenever assessment is brought to bear, I become personally engaged. Assessment or judgment is far from a detached process of checking or comparing. It reaches to my roots as a person-in-the-world, with a past and a future.

This does not mean, however, that every statement entertained for verification must have some palpably practical effect. In spite of the accepted connotations of "pragmatism," the criteria which I have assimilated from Dewey need not be freighted in an activist way. If we are speaking of Newton's laws, then acknowledging their truth means, above and beyond accepted verification, recognizing the demand we have for simple and coherent explanation, and quite simply submitting to their sway when they are operative in my own life. If, on the other hand, it is something to be done, then acknowledging the truth of the proposal means committing myself to its realization. Aristotle, we remember, insisted that a practical syllogism concludes not to a statement but to an action. More refinedly, to assent to the syllogism in such a way as to draw the conclusion is to intend to carry out the activity envisaged.

Why commit oneself? Because if I did not, I could not live with myself. The proposals which have given shape to my life to date already point me to a certain kind of future. To the extent that they have given a certain fullness and consistency to my life, I cannot but recognize their truth. Hence a policy which promises to continue and deepen that line of development can only be seen as contributing to a more genuine *me*. Of course, "contributing to a more genuine *me*" cannot be considered a criterion in any strict sense of the term. In fact, one of the criteria for a course of action that contributes to my own genuineness is precisely an increased appreciation of the paradoxes latent in the language used to describe our criteria of judgment. A proposal which promises to be *fruitful* must also be *discriminating,* and one which is unifying cannot fail to acknowledge nuances and differences. By "appreciating the paradoxes in the language" I mean to imply a certain attunement of the person with the norms he is using—the sort of thing which poetry, art and music attempt to *effect* in the viewer or listener. Part of this attunement lies in personally realizing the patent linguistic fact that norms do not function like standards. Another part is to recognize how invoking norms implies a decision to live, think and experience in fidelity to them.

This final point brings our circuitous argument full circle. To make assessments is to live with the decisions we make. It implies accepting into our lives the personal consequences of the norms employed. This is the consistency required of judgment. And without it there is no distinct activity worthy of the name, nothing more than an inflexible "application" of a preconceived pattern. So we can see how implementing the unrestricted desire to know goes hand in glove with allowing the unrestricted desire to *be* full scope in our lives.

It is our reflective wonder at this vast interior world that opens us out beyond the consistency of formal systems, puts us in contact with ourselves and readies us to receive as a gift the utterly paradoxical unification which is faith. For *faith* in this context is simply the enduring assurance that there *is* someone to be faithful to, that there is a *myself*. In practice, this means acknowledging all the barriers that I keep placing to a life lived in communion with the world and myself, yet allowing this me-cum-barriers to be acknowledged and accepted for what it is. This acceptance is the gift unwarranted and inexplicable. And permitting it to occur is also a gift. The Christian *is* the humanist who trusts his ground, but trust is not something achieved. It can only be bestowed.

NOTES

[1] Sören Kierkegaard, *Concluding Unscientific Postscript* (Princeton: Princeton University Press, 1941), p. 182.

[2] Sören Kierkegaard, *Sickness Unto Death* (Garden City: Doubleday, 1954), p. 147.

[3] John Dewey, *Experience and Nature*, 2nd ed. (New York: Dover, 1926), p. 8.

⁴ C. S. Peirce, *Collected Papers* (Cambridge, Mass.: Belknap Press, 1934), p. 113.

SUGGESTED READING

Haughton, Rosemary. *Transformation of Man* (Springfield, Illinois: Templegate, 1967).

Moore, Sebastian. *God Is a New Language* (Glen Rock, New Jersey: Newman, 1967).

Novak, Michael. *Belief and Unbelief* (New York: New American Library, 1967).

Ogden, Shubert. *Reality of God* (New York: Harper and Row, 1966).

DOMINIC M. CROSSAN, O.S.M.

Eschatological Statements
in the New Testament

REV. DOMINIC M. CROSSAN, O.S.M., a member of the Servite Fathers, provides a brilliant sample of biblical exegesis as his contribution to the theme, The Future as the Presence of Shared Hope. Under the subject "Eschatological Statements in the New Testament," he explores both the depth and breadth of the "little apocalypse" of Mark 13, as one example of New Testament eschatology.

Although a young theologian, Father Crossan has already distinguished himself as teacher and author. He has served as Professor of Sacred Scripture at Stonebridge Priory, Illinois; at St. Norbert Abbey, Wisconsin; at Barat College, Chicago; at Loyola University, Chicago; and at St. Mary's College, Indiana. Currently, he is Professor of Biblical Theology at St. Mary of the Lake Seminary, Illinois.

Father Crossan has written *The Literary Structure of Mark* (publication pending); *The Gospel of Eternal Life* (Milwaukee: Bruce, 1966); *Scanning the Sunday Gospel* (Milwaukee: Bruce, 1965); and numerous articles, including "Mary and the Church in John 1:13," *Bible Today*, 20 (November 1965); "Anti-Semitism and the Gospel," *Theological Studies*, 26 (June 1965); and "The Biblical Poetry of the Hebrews," *Bible Today*, 13 (October 1964).

Two years' recent experience at École Biblique, Jerusalem, added first-hand archeological investigations and textual studies to his rich background.

THE DIFFICULTY with this subject is not primarily its expansive scope nor even the fact that the entire discussion of New Testament eschatology seems as wide open today as it ever has been. It is true that items basic to such a synthesis are still considerably controverted, for example, the title Son of Man[1] or the theme of the Kingdom of God.[2] It is equally true that the New Testament teaching on eschatology is neither pure imminent apocalypse[3] nor as yet total realized exchatology[4] but rather a dialectic in which these two extremes and their many tones are held in mutual tension and tide.[5] The real difficulty is that there seems to have been a serious methodological flaw in the past investigation of such wide-ranging themes as eschatology.

This error in methodology can be shown clearly from a consideration of the apocalyptic discourse in Mk 13, Mt 24-25, and Lk 21. Consider two methods of handling these texts. In one method the three accounts are studied in more or less parallel columns in their so-called "synoptic relations," and the study might be termed something like "The Synoptic Apocalypse" or "The Eschatology of the Synoptic Gospels." But something very important tends to be obscured, if not lost, in such a method, namely, the dialectical tension whereby biblical truth is ordinarily conveyed. Similarities are stressed and divergences tend to be erased. But above all, one fundamental difference is not even considered. How does the position of these chapters within the individual structure and theology of their respective authors change their whole aspect from within, from a depth far below questions of parallel phrases or similar sentences?

The other method seems to obviate this problem. It demands that Mk 13, for example, be considered within the overall structure and theology of Mark, that the same be done for Mt 24-25 and for Lk 21, and that these be securely fixed in their own proper individuality before any attempt is made at comparisons. In other words, for this methodology questions of literary structure must precede decisions on theological content, problems of thought and interpretation must be handled within an investigation of overall form and general construction. If we are to find the author's mind and intention rather than seek confirmation of our own preconceived theories, we must discipline our exegesis in the same way he had to discipline his composition—by form and structure for him, by the study of that form and structure for us.

The purpose of this study is to offer a new investigation of one major element of New Testament eschatology within the rubrics of the methodology just advocated. It is really an experiment and an exercise in methodology with emphasis on form as the key to content, structure as the handmaid of theology. The section to be studied is the "little apocalypse" of Mk 13, and this will be treated against the background of the overall construction of Mark's gospel and the basic theological vision therein contained. This subject is obviously much more limited than the title of this chapter indicates. But the method will be much more scientific and objective and the results therefore much more valid and enduring.

I. THE STRUCTURE OF MARK 13

The formal structure of Mk 13, 1-37 will first be studied to insure that the content intended by Mark as well as the priorities and emphases intended by him are objectively discovered.[6] After setting the scene outside the Temple in the first two verses and the question of the disciples in verses 3 and 4 the discourse falls into three main sections: the signs preceding the advent of the Son of Man in verses 5-23; the advent itself and the ingathering of the elect in verses 24-27; and the questions of day and hour and time in verses 28-37. Throughout this analysis the prime discipline of the method is the use of objective word-indices in the text. The reconstruction will be based solely on such criteria of form rather than on content.

A. THE CONSTRUCTION OF 13, 5-23

The first section that distinguishes itself as a literary unit runs from verse 5 to verse 23. The inaugural question of the disciples is "Tell us . . . all things," the opening and closing words of verse 4. In verse 23 Jesus concludes the section with, "I have foretold you all things." In this integrated unit marked apart as a literary unit by these verbal indices, there are five elements in a chiastic structure which we shall examine.

1. *13, 5-6 and 13, 21-23*

(5) And Jesus began to say to them, "Take heed that no one leads you astray.

(6) Many will come in my name, saying, 'I am he!' and they will lead many astray.

(21) And then if anyone says to you, 'Look, here is the Christ!' or 'Look, there he is!' do not believe it.

(22) False Christs and false prophets will arise and show signs and wonders, to lead astray, if possible, the elect.

(23) But take heed; I have told you all things beforehand."[7]

Both the first and final elements refer to false Messiahs who attempt to deceive the followers of Jesus. The first opens with "Be on your guard"[8] (13,5) and the latter closes with it, "Be on your guard" (13,23). Both pericopes couch their warnings against such deception with the phrase, "one of you" (13, 5.21). Finally the verb "to deceive" appears in simple form in 13,5.6 and in a compound form in 13,22.

2. *13, 7-8 and 13, 14-20*

(7) "And when you hear of wars and rumors of wars, do not be alarmed; this must take place, but the end is not yet.

(8) For nation will rise against nation, and kingdom against kingdom; there will be earthquakes in various places; there will be famines; this is but the beginning of the sufferings.

(14) But when you see the desolating sacrilege set up where it ought not to be (let the reader understand), then let those who are in Judea flee to the mountains;

(15) let him who is on the housetop not go down, nor enter his house, to take anything away;

(16) and let him who is in the field not turn back to take his mantle.

(17) And alas for those who are with child and for those who give suck in those days!

(18) Pray that it may not happen in winter.

(19) For in those days there be such tribulation as has not been from the beginning of the creation which God created until now, and never will be.

(20) And if the Lord had not shortened the days, no human being would be saved; but for the sake of the elect, whom he chose, he shortened the days."

Once again we have two parallel pericopes, and, as in the previous instance, the second is much more detailed. The former begins with "When you hear" (13,7) and the latter with "When you see" (13,14). The former two parallel pericopes dealt with Messianic deception, and those two parallel units deal with terrible human suffering.

3. 13, 9-13

(9) "But take heed to yourselves; for they will deliver you to councils; and you will be beaten in synagogues; and you will stand before governors and kings for my sake, to bear testimony before them.

(10) And the gospel must be preached to all nations.

(11) And when they bring you to trial and deliver you up, do not be anxious beforehand what you are to say; but say whatever is given you in that hour, for it is not you who speak, but the Holy Spirit.

(12) And brother will deliver up brother to death, and the father his child, and children will rise against parents and have them put to death;

(13) and you will be hated by all for my name's sake. But he who endures to the end will be saved."

This is the hinge of the chiastic construction. It is the formal center of the section and therefore the most important part of its content as far as Mark is concerned. Within these verses Mark has forged another smaller chiasm between the three statements of verses 9 and 10, verse 11, and verses 12 and 13. Each statement contains a single use of a very important key-word of Mark's whose function will be seen more fully later. This is the term "hand over" in verses 9, 11 and 12.

In the balanced statements of 13, 9-10 and 13, 12-13 four similar points are touched upon. In verses 9-10 their "handing over" will be "to sanhedrins; you will be beaten in syna-gogues," that is, they will appear before the spiritual authori-ties. But also, "you will stand before governors and kings," that is they will also be summoned before the civil powers. Secondly, all this will happen "for my sake," for the sake of Jesus. Thirdly, their presence will "bear witness" to both the powers involved: the spiritual ("them") and the temporal ("all the nations").[9] Fourthly, there is mention of time: "The Good News must first be proclaimed." In 13, 12-13 these same four points are taken up again. Now their "handing over" is "to death." This happens again for the sake of Jesus, "on ac-count of my name." Once again the universal note is struck in, "you will be hated by all men." Finally, the element of time reappears with, "the man who stands firm to the end will be saved." From these formal characteristics it follows that verse 11 is the heart of 13, 9-13 which is itself the center of 13, 5-23. This verse promises to the disciples that the gospel will first be preached before their time of "handing over" arrives and that they will have the presence of the Holy Spirit under trial.[10]

B. THE VISION OF 13, 24-27

(24) "But in those days, after that tribulation, the sun will be darkened, and the moon will not give its light,

(25) and the stars will be falling from heaven, and the powers in the heavens will be shaken.

(26) And then they will see the Son of man coming in clouds with great power and glory.

(27) And then he will send out the angels, and gather his elect from the four winds, from the ends of the earth to the ends of heaven."

This next element presents a very difficult structural problem. On the one hand, it is clearly outside the chiastic balance of verses 5-23; and neither does it pertain to the equally closed chiastic parallel of verses 28-37. On the other hand, there are clear word-links between this unit and the preceding two sections, 13, 14-20 and 21-23. In the first we had the sequence: "in those days . . . distress . . . the elect"; and in verses 21-23 "the elect" appears again. Then in verses 24-27 there is again the repetition of "in those days . . . distress . . . the elect" in the same order.[11] These verbal links between these two sections, and especially the mention of "distress" and "after that time of distress," must mean that the two units of 13,5-23 and 24-27, while separated structurally, are also closely associated. But for the moment 13,24-27, the vision of the Son of Man's advent and the angelic ingathering of the elect, must remain formally poised between the chiastically closed units of 13,5-23 just studied and 13,28-37 now to be investigated.

C. THE CONSTRUCTION OF *13, 28-37*

The structure is exactly parallel to that of verses 5-23. There are five elements in chiastic balance, and we must once again study their individual elements.

1. *13, 28-29 and 13, 33, 37*

(28) "From the fig tree learn its lesson: as soon as its branch becomes tender and puts forth its leaves, you know that summer is near.

(29) So also, when you see these things taking place, you know that he is near, at the very gates.

(33) Take heed, watch; for you do not know when the time will come.

(34) It is like a man going on a journey, when he leaves home and puts his servants in charge, each with his work, and commands the doorkeeper to be on the watch.

(35) Watch therefore—for you do not know when the master of the house will come, in the evening, or at midnight, or at cockcrow, or in the morning—

(36) lest he come suddenly and find you asleep.

(37) And what I say to you I say to all: Watch."

Both these elements contain parables, that of the fig tree in the former and that of the returning master in the latter. They are composed in similar structure: three sets of imperatives serve as frames for two notes of time which are placed in between them, as follows:

13, 28-29	13, 33-37
"learn"	"stay awake"
"when" (*'otan*)	"when" (*pote*)
"know"	"watch"
"when" (*'otan*)	"when" (*pote*)
"know"	"watch"

This parallel in structure draws immediate attention to the two indications of time, for which different words are used in Greek: *'otan* and *pote*. The former word is used quite frequently in Mark and is in no way exceptional. The word *pote* appears as such only in 13,4 besides the verses we are now examining. It is the sequence of Mark's usage of these two words within the framework of 13,1-37 which is striking. Both words appear in the original question of 13,4, "tell us, when (*pote*) is this going to happen, and what sign will there be when (*'otan*) all things are about to be fulfilled?" Then in the five balanced elements of 13,5-23 *'otan* appears in the parallel verses 7 and 14 around the central usage in verse 11. Finally, in the concluding section of 13, 28-37 each word is used twice, and in mutual parallel, but in reverse sequence (*'otan, pote*) to the opening order in the question of verse 4 (*pote, 'otan*). From this one would conclude that the *pote* and *'otan* of 13,4 are being distinguished deliberately by Mark in 13,28-29 and 13,33-37. In the first parable the time element is somewhat defined. The, "when (*'otan*) you see these things happening" (13,29) recalls the "when" (*'otan*) of verses 7, 11 and 14, and says that when all this occurs they must know that the event described in verses 24-27 is "at the very gates." But in the second parable, verses 33-37, the time element is twice declared to be unknown: "you do not know when (*pote*)" in verses 33 and 35. It is not possible for these two passages, 13,28-29 and 13,33-37, to refer to the same moment of the same event.

2. 13, 30, 31 *and* 32

(30) "Truly, I say to you, this generation will not pass away before all these things take place.

(31) Heaven and earth will pass away, but my words will not pass away.

(32) But of that day or that hour no one knows, not even the angels in heaven, nor the Son, but only the Father."

The next parallel elements explicitly discuss this question of time. The first element in verse 30 is a continuation of verses 28-29: the "when . . . happens" (*genētai*) of verse 28 leads into the "when . . . these things happening" of the next verse and then into the "all these things will have happened" (*genētai*) of verse 30. This final, "all these things" recalls the original "all . . . these things" of the end of verse 4. When what is described in verses 5-23 happened they would know that the events of verses 24-27 were very near. Similarly, the second note of time in verse 32 is in line with verses 33-37, the "nobody knows" reflecting the "you do not know" of that section. The "when" (*pote*) of verses 4, 33 and 35 belongs exclusively to the Father.

The time element stated in verses 28-30 dates the signs described in verses 5-23 within the audience's lifetime; but the time element in verses 32 to 37 carefully refuses any precise knowledge for the time of the appearance of the Son of Man. One other element is equally clear. While denying exact knowledge of this time, Mark certainly expects it to happen soon after the signs described in the preceding section. We admit that we do not know the time of eschatological fulfillment, but we presume it is long away. Mark admits that he does not know that date either, but presumes that it is very soon. We might establish the following equation. The preceding signs of verses 5-23 are dated within the generation of Jesus' audience; but the eschatological Event of verses 24-27 is refused any dating. But once again it must be emphasized that such refusal of precise dating is not incompatible with a hope that it is extremely imminent.

In the center of the chiasm of verses 28-37 stands verse 31, the solemn assurance that Jesus' words will come true. Because of its position this assurance would refer both to the known time element in verses 28-30 and the unknown time element in verses 32-37.

The construction of the discourse in Mk 13,1-37 is clearly a five-element chiasm including the preceding signs, the time element and a central climactic element in verses 24-27. Only after this carefully constructed unit is replaced in the total structure of Mark can any investigation of its theology be legitimately undertaken.

II. THE TOTAL STRUCTURE OF MARK

This treatment will follow the same objective methodology of seeking Mark's intention from indices in the formal details of the text itself. The thesis is that Mark's overall construction comprises three great narrative cycles: A. The First or Inaugural Cycle is that of John the Baptist, in 1,1-15. B. The Second Cycle is that of Jesus himself, in 1,16-8,26 and 8,27-16,8. C. The Third or Eschatological Cycle appears as prophetic promise within the two halves of this Second Cycle in 6,7-30 and 13,1-37.

A. THE FIRST OR INAUGURAL CYCLE

The opening unit of chapter 1, verses 1-15, is not only the first complex, it is an inaugural one. Its overall structure establishes in miniature the basic sequence of the far larger complex of chapter 1, verse 16, to chapter 16, verse 8. It can be demonstrated that this opening section extends to verse 15[12] and not just to either verse 8[13] or 13,[14] as has been contended.

The term "Good News" appears only seven times in all of Mark. Three of these are here, and one is immediately arrested by its use in the very first line, "the beginning of the Good News," and then the repeated, "Good News from God," in verse 14 and, "believe the Good News" in verse 15. This term will not appear again until chapter 8, verse 35, and then later in 10,29; 13,10; and 14,9. This serves as an index of inclusion to set apart, at least as a working hypothesis, 1,1-15 as the primal unit to be considered. A similar but secondary inclusion may be present between the "of God" of verse 1[15] and the repeated "of God" in verses 14 and 15. These are the first three uses of "God" in Mark. Within the framework of 1,1-15 the narrative falls easily into three sections as the twice repeated, "It happened that" of verses 4 and 9 divides the text. In verses 1-3 we have the Old Testament linkage and overture. Then verses 4-8 concern John the Baptist while verses 9-13 turn rather to Jesus. More precisely these last two sections discuss respectively: (a) the mission of John (1,4-8); and (b) the transition from John to Jesus (1,9-15). The former point is quite simple. It details briefly the mission of John which is strictly for Israel: "All Judaea and the people of Jerusalem made their way to him" (1,5a). But the second point is more important. It is characterized by a journey which is reversed after the "handing over" (*paradidōmi*) of John: (1) "Jesus came from Nazareth in Galilee" (1,9); (2) "after John had been handed over" (1,14a); (3) "Jesus went into Galilee" (1,14b). We have accordingly the *mission* of John in 1,4-8 and the *transition* from John to Jesus in 1,9-15. This transition has three component elements: a journey from north to south, the "handing over" of John, and the reversal of the preceding journey, now back from south to north.

B. THE SECOND CYCLE

The same balance of mission and transition and the same internal pattern of the transition's elements can be seen in the second cycle, that of Jesus himself.

1. The Mission (1,16-8,26)

In 1,16-8,26 the general emphasis is on Jesus' mission to the people. The Twelve are with him most of the time, but there is an obvious lack of equality in their participation. After the initial section in 1,16-3,12 establishes the main structural themes to be developed,[16] the two blocks of 3,13-6,56 and 7,1-8,26 show this ministry as being, at least in prophetic promise, for both Israel and the nations respectively.[17]

2. The Transition (8,27-16,8)

Then in 8,27-16,8 the focus changes from mission to transmission, from ministry to transition, but this transition is now from Jesus to the Twelve. The most striking point is that the transition again takes place under the same three rubrics as seen previously in 1,9-15: (1) the journey from north to south; (2) the "handing over" of the one whose mission is under discussion; (3) the return from south to north of those who now take up the mission in their turn.

(a) *The Journey from Galilee.* The southward journey starts from even farther north than Galilee itself. In 8,27 Jesus and the Twelve are in "the villages around Caesarea Philippi." In 9,30 they start southward, "leaving that place they made their way through Galilee," and in 9,33, "they came to Capernaum." In 10,1 they are farther south again, "Leaving there, he came to the district of Judaea, beyond the Jordan." For the first time the terminus of the journey is explicitly stated to be "to Jerusalem" twice in 10,32.33. Mention of Jerusalem has been deliberately omitted before this for reasons of structure and emphasis. Mark intended to use the phrase "to Jerusalem" seven times for Jesus' last journey. Elsewhere he only uses the town's name three times and always as "from Jerusalem" as friends (3,8) or enemies (3,22; 7,1) come to Galilee for him. These are now the first two of seven uses of "to Jerusalem" as Jesus approaches the place of his destiny.[18]

(b) *The "Handing Over" of Jesus.* The verb "to hand over" (*paradidōmi*) in this inimical sense is one of the most important structural terms in Mark. It is used for the fate of the Baptist in 1,14, and then 14 times for Jesus, twice seven uses: 3,19, the prophecy of Judas' betrayal; 9,31; 10,33ab, the prophecies of Jesus' destiny; 14,10.11.18.21.41.42.44, the realization of Judas' betrayal; 15,1.10.15, the fulfillment of the prophecies of final "handing over."[19] We have also seen the triple usage of this verb for the fate of the Twelve in 13,9-13 and this will be seen again later. The verb is never used in this hostile sense of other individuals in Mark.[20] The point is quite clear. The journey of Jesus from Galilee to Jerusalem is to conclude with the "handing over" of Jesus.

(c) *The Return to Galilee.* The first mention of a reversal of the journey is in 14,28. In 14,26-28 there is a prophecy of the failure of all the disciples but of the ultimate victory of

Jesus and of their own restoration. The verb "to go before" is used by Mark of Jesus only three times; and only twice more of others. Its use in 10,32 makes it clear that we are dealing there and in 14,28 with a deliberately reversed journey and not merely two disparate pieces of topography: "going up to Jerusalem, Jesus was going before them" (10,32) and, "I shall go before you to Galilee" (14,28). The journey foretold in 14,28 is intended by Mark as a deliberate reversal of that told in 10,32.

Between the promised "going before" of 14,28 and its ful-fillment in 16,7 occurs, almost in passing, a phrase which links together for the first and only time the two precise termini of the journey. In the Greek the structure of the verse tends to stress the two places: "in Galilee . . . followed him . . . served him . . . went up with him . . . to Jerusalem." This is an added confirmation of Mark's deliberate intent of stressing a reversed journey.

But of all the verses which mention the reversed journey 16,7 is the most important because of its climactic and closing position. It also has striking connections with 10,32-34, and not only in the repetition of the verb "to go before" for Jesus. In both cases there is also the mention of awe and fear, and this is rather inexplicable as stated in 10,32. It is intended to warn the reader that the journey is not just a change in geo-graphical location but denotes the awesome and fearful transi-tion which takes place through the "handing over" of Jesus.

The transition from Jesus to the disciples in the Second Cycle follows the same pattern as that from John to Jesus in the First Cycle, but on a much larger scale. Mission gives way to tran-sition, and this latter takes place as a "handing over" which happens at the turning point of the journey which comes from north to south and then returns from south to north.

C. THE THIRD OR ESCHATOLOGICAL CYCLE

After consideration of the first and second cycles two questions immediately pose themselves. First, what would Mark's readers think of the events between 16,7-8 and their own day? How could Mark end like this without at least some injunction to a world-wide mission such as Matthew appends to his account, or some substitute for the full second volume which Luke found necessary for his record?[21] Secondly, what does all the insistence on Galilee really mean? If the pattern established by the two previous cycles was to be continued, then (1) the return to Galilee of 16,7 should beget a new outward journey; (2) the protagonists of this third cycle would be the disciples and Peter, taking over in their turn from Jesus as he had from John; (3) eventually a "handing over" might be expected from them; (4) and the new and successive protagonist would take over his mission in turn. Otherwise one would have to say that the cyclic pattern just argued for is of very minor importance and little more than a structural nicety. We know what happened when Jesus returned alone to Galilee in 1, 14-15, but what happened when the Risen Lord went before the disciples back to Galilee in 16,7? The hypothesis here advanced is that a third cycle is present in Mark but that it appears as a prophecy in the two halves of the cycle of Jesus previously discussed. The future mission is promised in 6,7-30, while the future transition is promised in 13,1-37. This is termed the third or eschatological cycle, and it should be noted immediately that it has the same twin elements of mission and transition already seen in the cycles of John (1,1-15) and Jesus (1,16-16,8).

1. The Prophecy of Mission in 6, 7-30

The narrative in 6,7-30 is puzzling on both historical and literary levels. How exactly does Mark, who alone insists so unremittingly on their incomprehension, explain such a successful apostolic mission as here recorded? As soon after it as 6,52 he uses for the Twelve a term reserved by other New Testament writers to describe rooted opposition to truth: "hardened heart."[22] Secondly, why does he spoil his own careful literary activity by recounting in detail (6,14-29) the death of John when the cycle of the Baptist had been closed with 1,1-15? It is not a question of mentioning John, which is done again in 8,28 and 11,30-33, but of detailing what had already been included and concluded with his single terse "handing over" in 1,14.

(*a*) *The Baptist and Jesus.* Mark recounts the fate of the Baptist in 6,14-29 with phrases deliberately similar to the terms he will later use for the last days of Jesus' life, with regard to John's "resurrection" (6,14-16), death (6,17-28) and burial (6,29).

(*1*) *Resurrection: John and Jesus* (6,14-16). Mark goes out of his way to stress the theme of John's resurrection, of Jesus as the risen Baptist:

"Herod heard . . . and said[23] . . . John has risen from the dead . . .
   Others said . . .
   Others said . . .
Herod heard . . . and said . . . John has risen from the dead."

This contrasts, for example, with chapter 8, verse 28, where the three same possibilities are cited but with no explicit mention of resurrection and therefore no repetition of it. The emphasis on the resurrection of John belongs to Mark alone, and so do the parallel frames in which this emphasis is couched.

One other small point is worth noting. Mark never mentions what Herod "heard." In the parallels, Matthew has "Herod the Tetrarch heard about the reputation of Jesus," and Luke writes, "Herod the Tetrarch had heard about all that was going on." Mark does not use Jesus' name but leaves him at best implicit in the "him" of verse 14. For Mark's purpose the emphasis must remain on the "resurrection" of John and hence his fame and his wonders (6,14).

(2) *Death: John and Jesus* (6,17-28). There are six deliberate contacts between the manner in which John's fate is recorded and the narrative of Jesus' death in Mark. It should be noted that these resemblances all occur in 6,17-21a and stop at precisely the point when the death itself is engineered.

(a) 6,17a. It was noted earlier that Mark used the verb "to hand over" once for the fate of John and twice seven times for that of Jesus. Similar numerical structures are found here. The verb "to hold" (*krateō*) in the inimical sense of restraint is reserved by Mark once for John, here, and seven times for Jesus (3,21; 12,12; 14,1.44.46.49.51). (b) 6,16b. In the same way that John is "bound" in 6,17b Jesus is later "bound" by the authorities (15,1). (c) 6,19. The use of the verb, "to kill," for John and Jesus is similar to that just seen for the verb "to hold." Used here of John, it is used seven times for Jesus in 8,31; 9,31 (twice); 10,34; 12,7.8; and 14,1. (d) 6,20a. Even apart from specific words the general similarity of the two situations is clear. Herodias wishes to kill John but cannot because Herod fears him; some of the authorities wish to destroy Jesus but are likewise restrained because of their fear. In the case of the Baptist, "Herod was afraid of John" (6,20a).

With regard to Jesus his enemies hold their hand because, "they were afraid of him" (11,18). Actually they do not fear Jesus himself, as is explained by the immediately appended explanation, "because the people were carried away by his teaching." When the subject next arises this is stated more simply and precisely with "they were afraid of the crowds, so they left him alone and went away" (12,12). But the value of 11,18 is that it places their fear of Jesus in better parallel and linkage with Herod's fear of John himself. In both cases fear makes the enemy hold off on final action. (e) 6,20b. This phrase serves to continue the word-linkage with the fate of John and of Jesus. It is possibly the most interesting connection since a failure to realize its purpose has often forced commentators into romantic views of Herod sitting at John's feet in the dungeon. In this verse we are told that Herod "liked to listen to him" ('*ēdeōs aytoy ēkoyen*). With regard to Jesus, the authorities are forced to restrain their hostile intentions because the "people liked to listen to him" (*ēkoyen aytoy 'ēdeōs*) in 12,37b. The adverb '*ēdeōs* is only used in these two places by Mark, and only thrice more in the entire New Testament. There are not even similar ideas in the parallel passages in Matthew and Luke. (f) 6,21a. The word-links between the two deaths cease with the actual description of John's in 6,21b-28. But one last connection is forged. The desire of Herodias for revenge is foiled until a "suitable" (*eykairoy*) day arrives in 6,21a. When Judas offers to betray Jesus and the reward is promised he "looked for a way of betraying of him at a suitable time" (*eykairōs*) in 14,11. The adjectival form, *eykairoy*, is never again used by Mark. Neither does the adverbial form, *eykairōs*, ever appear again in Mark. Neither of the parallels (Mt 14,6 and Lk 3,19-20) have any mention of a suitable time.

(3) *Burial: John and Jesus* (6,29). The burial of John is told with "When John's disciples heard about this, they went and took his body (*to ptōma*) and laid it in a tomb" (6,29). After Jesus' death Joseph "went in" to Pilate, received *to ptōma* and "laid him in a tomb" (15,43-46). The important point here is not just the general similarity in both descriptions, which might be explained as a result of the similar situations. It is the word *to ptōma* for the dead body of Jesus which is most striking. This term was used for John's "corpse" in 6,29, but when Joseph addressed Pilate he first asked for "the body (*to sōma*) of Jesus." Only in the final clause, which must be parallel to John's case, does he use the more crude "the corpse" (*to ptōma*) for Jesus. Mark never uses *ptōma* elsewhere. In fact the term "corpse" (*ptōma*) appears elsewhere in the New Testament only in apocalyptic contexts. The use of the cruder word "corpse" (*ptōma*) instead of the more delicate one "body" (*sōma*) is a last deliberate link between the fate of John and that of Jesus.

(a) The Point of the Comparison. From the above analysis it is clear that the death-burial-"resurrection" of John the Baptist is told by Mark in terms similar to those later to be used for that of Jesus;[24] that "resurrection" is mentioned first; and that Jesus' name does not appear in the account. It is also striking that Mark reintroduces the Baptist's fate when it was already summed up in 1,14 within John's own cycle. Finally, there is the problem of an apparently successful mission by missionaries with hardened hearts. What exactly is the purpose and meaning of 6,7-30 and especially of the careful comparison of John and Jesus?

The solution proposed here is that Mark recorded the Galilean ministry after the death-burial-"resurrection" of John in such a way as to make it a prophetic cipher for the great world-wide mission of the Twelve after the death-burial-resurrection of Jesus himself. And that to draw attention forcibly to the linkage at the start he talked of Jesus as John redivivus before even discussing his death and burial. The account is not primarily interested in John and does not really pertain to either the first or second cycle, but represents the mission section of the third or eschatological cycle. The problem of missionary success by the uncomprehending preachers is not relevant to this section viewed in this way, since this Galilean activity is strictly a prophetic promise of the future.

But even apart from this comparison, Mark has carefully indicated his purpose in the general literary structure of 6,7-30. The actual "mission" of the Twelve is told as the frames of verses 7-13 and 30 for the discussion of the "resurrection"-death-burial of John in verses 14-29. This is done by an unusual literary flashback which is constructed so that the mission of the Twelve and the fate of John are intimately connected on the literary level. In itself John's fate reads as a literary postscript, but it is very important that the conclusion of the mission is recorded only after the full account of the fate of John-as-Jesus.[25]

2. *The Prophecy of Transition in 13, 1-37*

The cycles of John and Jesus were told under the general rubrics of mission and transition. The third or eschatological cycle finds its mission element in the prophecy of world-wide mandate in 6,7-30, and its transition element is found in the prophecy of consummation in 13,1-37. As in the preceding two cycles, we would expect that the transition element would mention "handing over" and reflect the theme of a journey reversed after this "handing over."

(a) *Transition by "Handing Over."* As for John and Jesus already, this transition must be through the "handing over" (*paradidōmi*) of the former "missioner." This is found in 13,9-13 which was the chiastic core and therefore most important element of the events and signs to precede the triumph of the Son of Man. It is indicative that our analysis of the structure of 13,1-37 led us to focus attention on this passage as being the most important preceding sign rather than on 13,14-20, which usually receives the burden of critical attention.[26] The triple use of the verb "to hand over" here has already been seen to be as deliberate as it was for John and Jesus. It is now their turn to pass through a similar fate. Those whose world-wide mission was prophesied in 6,7-30 have their consummation by "handing over" prophesied in 13,9-13. But this raises an even more important question: into whom or into what does this third transition take place? The transition by "handing over" of John led into the mission of Jesus and that of Jesus led into the mission of the Twelve, but what future lies ahead of the Twelve's "handing over"? How does the mission of the disciples have a transition and to whom or to what does it lead?

We saw already that Mark had two moments of time under discussion in 13,28-37, one known and one unknown. The events of 13,5-23 are timed, "before this generation has passed away all these things will have taken place" (13,30). But God alone knows the secret of the moment set afterwards for 13,24-27: "nobody knows it" (13,32), "you never know when" (13,33-35). The third or eschatological cycle is thus the last great sweep of Mark's vision of human history. "After" the "handing over" of the disciples their mission will pass into the hands of the eschatological Son of Man. One is convinced that Mark expected this to happen very soon "after," even while solemnly asserting that nobody knew exactly when. But what is important is that the transition of the third cycle, like that of the former two, likewise takes place by a "handing over," which is not failure but success, not merely the end of the Apostolic mission but the inauguration of the eschatological triumph of the Son of Man.

(b) *The Reversed Journey*. The transition through "handing over" of the other two cycles took place within the framework of a journey from Galilee and back again. Is there any such reversed journey possible for the eschatological cycle? Mark shows two aspects of this theme in the final cycle, what might be termed the real journey and the symbolic journey.

(1) *The Real Journey*. It was noted earlier that the prophecy of Apostolic "handing over" in 13,9-13 is structured in the form of a small chiasm: (a) 13,9-12; (b) 13,11; (a') 13,12-13. It was also noted that the two parallel sections, verses 9-10 and 12-13, have each four parallel points. We are here interested only in the second of these. This is the note of universality struck by "as a witness to them and to all the nations" (13,10), and again, "you will be hated by all men" (13,13).[27] In both cases this universality presumes a world-wide mandate and therefore a real journey without limitation of place, a journey "to all the nations." The reversal of this journey is seen in the ingathering of the elect before the throne of the eschatological Son of Man. In the vision of 13,24-27 the Son of Man, "will send the angels to gather his chosen from the four winds, from the ends of the earth to the ends of heaven" (13,27). One feature of this Old Testament quotation is worth noting, the words "of the earth." The ordinary idiom

is either, "from the end of heaven to the end of heaven" (Dt 30,4) or, "from the end of the earth to the end of the earth" (Dt 13,8). But the word "earth" in Mk 13,27b seems to have been deliberately forced into the Old Testament idiom by Mark. The linked journey outwards to all the nations in Mk 13,9-13 and the return of the elect to the triumphant Son of Man from the ends of the earth in 13,24-27 is Mark's reversed journey for the third or eschatological cycle.

(2) *The Symbolic Journey.* It was noted already that at the end of the second cycle of Mark's construction the Risen Lord reversed his journey and returned to Galilee. The command was given, "You must go and tell his disciples and Peter, 'He is going before you to Galilee; it is there you will see him, just as he told you'" (16,7). Such a geographical return was demanded by the cyclic pattern of the structure, and 16,7 must be taken first of all as the ending of the second cycle, the cycle of Jesus, in 1,16-16,8. But by the logic of the structural rhythm Galilee must also be the starting point of the third cycle, and, being its beginning, must also be its end. That is, the term and the place, "Galilee," is becoming a cipher for the cyclic or dynamic nature of this historic process from John to eschaton. The term is a symbol of departure and return, of end as new beginning, and of the onward and eschatological thrust of mission.

The idea that Galilee is not just a place for Mark but has been elevated to the role of symbol is well known. In general, two main opinions on the content of the symbol have emerged. Ignoring their nuances for the moment, these explain Galilee as the place-symbol for mission to the world,[28] or as the place-cipher for eschatological consummation, for Parousia.[29] Both explanations are true, but only if taken together. This is not said as an attempt at syncretism or compromise, but as a necessary corollary from the cyclic pattern of beginning and ending in Galilee. The third cycle began in Galilee (world mission) and must end "in" Galilee (the Parousia) as well. This is not a crude attempt to locate the eschaton in place, somewhere in the hills or plains of Galilee. It is a literary way of stressing the unity and finality of the entire process, the cyclic symbolism which bespeaks the will and the control of God.

The message of 16,7 was, "He is going before you to Galilee; it is there you will see him, just as he told you." It is clear that this "He is going before you" of 16,7 fulfills the promise "after my resurrection I shall go before you to Galilee" of 14,28. But where was it ever foretold to them that "it is there you will see him"? The form used for the verb in "there you will see him" (*opsesthe*) recalls the only two previous uses of this form (13,26 and 14,62) which both refer to the ultimate triumph in Parousia of the Son of Man. It would seem from this formal connection that Mark wishes us to associate the vision of the eschatological Son of Man in 13,26 and 14,62 with the sight of the Risen Lord in 16,7. In other words, the final vision of the Son of Man at his Parousia is foretold for all in 13,26, which includes both his enemies in 14,62, and his friends in 16,7. The proposed interpretation of 16,7 can be summarized as follows. The verse has three sections: (a) "He is going before you to Galilee"; (b) "It is there you will see him"; (c) "just as he told you." The final statement refers back to *both* the preceding parts of the sentence. The "preceding" was foretold in 14,28 and its fulfillment represents the start of the third or eschatological cycle. The "seeing" was foretold in 13,26 and its fulfillment represents the end of the third or eschatological cycle, that is, the Parousia itself. The formal connection of these three passages is very important. If we only had 13,26 and 16,7 it might be argued that what was promised and fulfilled was a post-resurrectional apparition in Galilee. But his enemies will also see the promised vision as we know from 14,62, and no such enemy ever sees the Risen Lord. But both friends and enemies must alike face the eschatological Son of Man. It must be repeated that we are not dealing with any crude physical topography of the Parousia. To say that their mission starts from Galilee and that it will only end in Galilee at the Parousia is to stress the dynamic finality and essential continuity of the process, from the Risen Lord to the eschatological Son of Man. To locate the beginning and end "in" the same place is to emphasize the unity of the third cycle both in itself and in conjunction with the two preceding ones.

III. THE ESCHATOLOGY OF MARK

This chapter began by advocating a certain method of approach to themes which tended to range far across the New Testament writings and especially to ones that could easily be gathered up into facile synoptic generalizations. In order to study the eschatology of Mk 13 it argued for (1) the careful study of the form and structure of Mk 13 to see from constructional position what Mark really thought was central and what peripheral, what primary and what secondary in it; (2) the similar careful study of the overall structure of Mark's writing to see where this chapter fitted into its form and content. The underlying principle was quite simple. Only when theology was investigated in the light of structural literary analysis might one find Mark's thought as distinct from confirming our own ideas selectively from his text. Only after such a total view of Mark was obtained should comparisons be made with Matthew or Luke and, even then, only with texts of these writers already treated in the same way.

There is one point which tends to confirm the structural analysis of Mark's eschatology outlined above. It fits perfectly into the classical position on the date, place and occasion of the writing. In general the vast majority of commentaries agree with the ancient tradition that Mark is to be dated from Rome after the persecution of Nero and the martyrdom of Peter and Paul.[30] The shock of Nero's persecution had deeply affected the Roman community. There is evidence in Mark himself that all its members might not have been as steadfast as they should (4,17),[31] but that some had forgotten the destiny of persecution they should have been expecting (10,30).[32] Mark must compose a work which at once admonishes their failure and, more importantly, stimulates their hope and excites their expectation. He decided to compose his work in three great cycles. Each cycle would begin with mission and end in transition to the protagonist of the next cycle. The end would not be the end but a triumphant new beginning. This was the profound theological intuition which Mark offered as consolation to the Roman community in its hour of trial and persecution. The first cycle was that of John, and his transition to Jesus was signified by the key concepts of "handing over" and the reversed journey[33] (1,1-15). The next cycle would follow the same model. This is the cycle of Jesus and involves both his mission (1,16-8,26) and the transition by "handing over" during the reversed journey. This time the transition is to the Twelve, especially the inner Three, and most especially Peter himself (8,27-16,8). The last cycle takes the narrative from resurrection to Parousia, and the attention is on the disciples and especially Peter. Their mission is seen prophetically in 6,7-30, and reaches its consummation in the eschatological vision of 13,1-37. They too must suffer "handing over," and their going out to the ends of the earth would be reversed by the Son of Man who gathers them in as he comes in final victory and ultimate triumph. Standing at a moment of shock and consternation in the early church's history, bereft of the great figure of Peter, Mark speaks out in hope and expectation. This "handing over" of the Apostles is not the end but the beginning of the great final triumph of the Risen Lord. No doubt, Mark expected this to happen quite soon after his point of writing or else it would have been of scant consolation to those caught and shocked by Nero's persecution. But this "after" does not essentially affect the theology itself. The third cycle of Mark's narration has been expanded in time far beyond what he imagined. But his great central intuition speaks most assuredly to our present generation. He programmed his history in three cycles but used them to defend the theory that what seemed dissolution and defeat was actually triumphant new beginning. We may envisage a million cycles summarized in his great third, eschatological one. We see cycles of transition on the personal and ecclesial level, on the national and international scene, but Mark can still remind us forever that each new moment of time arises out of the ashes of the preceding one, and that those who cannot live with ashes cannot live in time. He reminds us that ideas and thoughts go into decline and that newer and better ones can be born from their departure. He reminds us above all that the moment when a community seems to be entering total dissolution may well be its moment of creative rebirth and renewed creation.

NOTES

1 A. Feuillet, "Le fils de l'homme de Daniel et la tradition biblique," *RB* 60 (1953) 170-202, 321-346; I. L. Sanders, "The Origin and Significance of the Title 'The Son of Man' as Used in the Gospels," *Script* 10 (1958) 49-56; T. A. Burkill, "The Hidden Son of Man in St. Mark's Gospel," *ZNW* 52 (1961) 189-213; J. Coppens, "Le fils d'homme daniélique et les relectures de Dan. VII, 13 dans les apocryphes et les écrits du Nouveau Testament," *ETL* 37 (1961) 5-51.

2 For the historical background on this theme cf. N. Perrin, *The Kingdom of God in the Teaching of Jesus* ("New Testament Library"; London, 1963).

3 On the thesis of A. Schweitzer cf. H. G. Wood, "Important and Influential Books—Albert Schweitzer and Eschatology," *ET* 65 (1953-4) 206-209; H. Schuster, "Die konsequente Eschatologie in der Interpretation des Neuen Testaments, kritisch betrachtet," *ZNW* 47 (1956) 1-25.

4 C. H. Dodd, *The Parables of the Kingdom* (3rd ed. rev.; London, 1961) and E. E. Wolfzorn, "Realized Eschatology. An Exposition of C. H. Dodd's Thesis," *ETL* 37 (1962) 44-62. Cf. also the critical reaction of J. A. McEvoy, "The Thesis of Realized Eschatology," *CBQ* 5 (1943) 396-407; "Realized Eschatology and the Kingdom Parables," *CBQ* 9 (1947) 329-357.

5 This dialectic and evolution is seen within the same literary work by M.-E. Boismard, "L'évolution du thème eschatologique dans les traditions johanniques," *RB* 68 (1961) 507-524.

6 This is the method used in the doctoral thesis summarized in J. Lambrecht, "Redactio Sermonis Eschatologi," *VD* 43 (1965) 278-287. His later publication, *Die Redaktion der Markus-Apokalypse* (Rome, 1967), was not available when this paper was written. Such preliminary structural analysis is lacking in other studies, for example, A. Feuillet, "Le discours de Jésus sur la ruine du Temple d'après Marc XIII et Luc XXI, 5-36," *RB* 55 (1948) 481-502; 56 (1949) 61-92.

7 *The Holy Bible, Revised Standard Version,* New York, Nelson, 1946, 1952. These verses from the gospel of Mark and the similar quotations which follow are from this version, copyrighted 1946 and 1952 by the Division of Christian Education of the National Council of Churches.

8 The author has supplied his own translation of biblical texts cited in his commentary because his argument depends on the structure given in the original Greek. Where the same Greek word is repeated in the original, he has repeated the English equivalent although such repetition may result in poor English style.

9 There is a problem in the Greek punctuation of 13,9-10. The division is here accepted as: . . . *eis martyrion aytois kai eis panta ta ethnē* (13,9-10a), and: *Prōton dei* . . . (13,10b). This is because of the parallel construction

between 13,9-10 and 12-13, and also because of the two steps (spiritual/temporal) of their "handing over" and concomitant witness. For critical discussion cf. G. D. Kilpatrick, "The Gentile Mission in Mark and Mark 13,9-11," *Studies in the Gospel* ("Essays in memory of R. H. Lightfoot"; Oxford, 1955) 145-158; disputed by A. Farrer, "An Examination of Mark XIII. 10," *JTS* 7 (1956) 75-79, and defended again in G. D. Kilpatrick, "Mark XIII.9-10," *JTS* 9 (1958) 81-86. On the textual problem of the verse cf. V. Taylor, *The Gospel according to St. Mark* (2nd ed.; London, 1966) 507; and earlier, C. H. Turner, "Marcan Usage: Notes, Critical and Exegetical, on the Second Gospel," *JTS* 26 (1925) 12-20 (cf. p. 20); P.-L. Couchoud, "Notes de critique verbale sur St. Marc et St. Matthieu," *JTS* 34 (1933) 113-138.

[10] The expression "in those days" appears only twice elsewhere in Mark (1, 9; 8, 1); but "distress" is only used in these two places and the similar context of 4, 17, while "the elect" never appears again outside 13, 20.22.27.

[11] In the same way an attack on Jesus in Mk 3,29 is an attack on the Holy Spirit.

[12] As indicated textually in *Grieches Neues Testament*, ed. H. F. von Soden (Göttingen, 1913) with the sub-title, "Die Vorgeschichte 1, 1-15." Objective criteria for this division are suggested by O. J. F. Seitz, "Praeparatio Evangelica in the Marcan Prologue," *JBL* 82 (1963) 201-206; "Gospel Prologues. A Common Pattern," *JBL* 83 (1964) 262-268. Cf. also L. E. Keck, "The Introduction to Mark's Gospel," *NTS* 12 (1965-6) 352-370 who maintains: "The real introduction to Mark is i.1-15" (p. 362), and M.-E. Boismard, "Evangile des Ebionites et problème synoptique," (Mc, 1,2-6 et par.), *RB* 73 (1966) 320-352 who argues for, "l'unite littéraire de Mc, 1,1-15" (p. 324).

[13] The break occurs here in the text of *The New Testament in the Original Greek*, eds. B. F. Westcott and F. J. A. Hort (London, 1892), and in *Novum Testamentum Graece*, eds. E. Nestle and K. Aland (25th ed.; Stuttgart, 1964).

[14] The first main division of *The Greek New Testament*, ed. R. V. G. Tasker (Oxford, 1964), the text followed in *The New English Bible* (Oxford, 1961). A similar break is argued by B. W. Bacon, "The Prologue of Mark: A Study of Sources and Structure," *JBL* 26 (1907) 84-106; C. H. Turner, "A Textual Commentary on Mark I," *JTS* 28 (1927) 145-158 reading *meta de* for *kai meta* in 1,14; R. H. Lightfoot, *History and Interpretation in the Gospels* (London, 1935) 61-66; H. Riesenfeld, "Tradition und Redaktion im Markusevangelium," *Neutestamentliche Studien für Rudolf Bultmann* (Berlin, 1954) 157-164.

[15] The reading *'yioy theoy* in 1,1 is accepted as original, cf. C. H. Turner, "Text of Mark I," *JTS* 28 (1927) 150-158; V. Taylor, *The Gospel according to St. Mark* (2nd ed,; London, 1966) 152.

16 These are four in number: the vocations, the teachings, the healings, and the mention of the crowds. All four themes are mentioned in two sets. The vocation of the four disciples in 1,16-20 preludes the teaching in 1,21-22 and is followed by four miracles in 1,23-28.29-31.40-45a; 2,3-12 and four mentions of the crowds in 1,32-39.45b; 2,1-2.13. Then the vocation of the single disciple in 2,14 leads into another teaching situation in 2,15-28 and this is followed by a single miracle in 3,1-6 and a concluding single mention of the crowds in 3,7-12.

17 This symbolism of the future mission of the Church to both Israel and the nations shown within the ministry of Jesus has been noted by T. A. Burkill, "Concerning Mk 5,7 and 5m18-20," *Studia Theologica* 11 (1957) 159-166; C. H. Cave, "The Obedience of Unclean Spirits," *NTS* 11 (1964-5) 93-97. This is especially evident in the twin multiplications of bread: cf. A. M. Farrer, "Loaves and Thousands," *JTS* 4 (1953) 1-14; F. W. Danker, "Mark viii 3," *JBL* 82 (1963) 215-216; B. van Iersel, "Die wunderbare Speisung und das Abendmahl in der synoptischen Tradition (Mk vi 35-44 par., viii 1-20 par.)," *NT* 7 (1964-5) 10-14.

18 The theme of the last journey to Jerusalem is well known in Luke but has not received sufficient emphasis in Mark. Cf. W. C. Robinson, Jr., "The Theological Context for Interpreting Luke's Travel Narrative (9:51 ff.)," *JBL* 79 (1960) 20-31.

19 The choice of *paradidōmi* to express the common fate of the Baptist, Jesus, and the disciples is most likely based on the use of this verb for the Servant of Yahweh in Is 53,12 (*paredothē* twice). This would certainly stress the Servant as a corporate entity for Mark.

20 Jn also uses the term with a certain solemnity and symbolism. It appears thirteen times for the "handing over" of Jesus himself: 6,64.71; 12,4; 13,2.11.21; 18,2.5.30.35.36; 19,11.16. The fourteenth use is climactic as Jesus "hands over" (*paredōken*) the spirit in death. It is Jesus who ultimately "hands over" himself to the will of God. This count ignores Jn 21,20.

21 This problem is discussed in J. M. Robinson, "Mark's Understanding of History," *ScotJT* 9 (1956) 393-409, expanded into *The Problem of History in Mark*, "Studies in Biblical Theology," No. 21; London, 1957. T. A. Burkill, "St. Mark's Philosophy of History," *NTS* 3 (1956-7) 142-148 distinguishes four periods: preparation, ministry, post-resurrectional period of gospel preaching, eschatological fulfilment (p. 143). This is developed at greater length in his *Mysterious Revelation. An Examination of the Philosophy of St. Mark's Gospel* (Ithica, N.Y., 1963).

22 In 6,52 and 8,17 Mark uses the term *pepōrōmenē(n)* for the disciples. There are no parallels for these in either Mt 14,33 or Mt 16,9=Lk 12,1. The verb *pōroō* is used five times in the NT, and in the other three it refers to those of Israel whose hearts are hardened (Jn 12,40; Rom 11,7; 2 Cor 3,14). Mark's use is quite deliberate and should not be mitigated in the

name of apostolic respect; cf. L. Cerfaux, "L'aveuglement d'esprit dans
l'évangile de Saint Marc," *Recueil Lucien Cerfaux* (Gembloux, 1954) II,
3-15.

[23] The majority of the witnesses read the singular (*elegen*) rather than the
plural (*elegon*) here. If Mark deliberately wanted to repeat the frames suggested here there is no reason to reject this majority reading. The *elegon*
plural could easily have arisen from assimilation to the two succeeding ones.

[24] J. Duncan M. Derrett, "Herod's Oath and the Baptist's Head," *BZ* 9 (1965)
49-59, 233-246 noted: "That the death of John was in some way explana-
tory of not only the movements of Jesus prior to his last journey to Jerusalem but also the behavior of the principal parties at the last, critical
moments of his life, seems highly likely, if not certain; but how precisely
it served to explain the latter has yet to be shown" (p. 239).

[25] I. de la Potterie, "Mors Johannis Baptistae (Mk 6,17-29)," *VD* 44 (1966)
142-151 has noted these same verbal links between the deaths and explained
it as John "praefigurans Christum" (p. 151). But the literary relationship
of 6,14-29 and 6,7-13.30 must also be considered, as well as the general
problem of the "third cycle" itself. Mk 6,14-29 is much more than an
artistically composed literary fill-in to separate departure (6,7-13) and return (6,30), despite E. von Dobschutz, "Zur Erzahlerkunst des Markus,"
ZNW 27 (1928) 193-198. C. W. F. Smith, "'Fishers of Men,'" *HarvTR*
52 (1959) 187-203: "The charge to the disciples (e.g., Mark 6:7-11 . . .)
is so clearly representative of a later situation that all traces of an earlier
mission (if it existed) which fits this call remain only as eschatological
fossils embedded in an account of the Christian mission" (p. 193-4).

[26] No doubt the form of the opening question in 13,4 after the situation and
comment of 13,1-2 dictate this emphasis on the ruin of the Temple. But
structure indicates that Mark is more interested in the death of the Apostles
than the ruin of Jerusalem as preparatory signs.

[27] On the punctuation of 13,10 cf. note 7 above.

[28] R. H. Lightfoot, *Locality and Doctrine in the Gospels* (London, 1938) 49-
65, 73-77, 106-126; G. H. Boobyer, "Galilee and Galileans in St. Mark's
Gospel," *BJRylL* 35 (1952-3) 334-348; C. F. Evans, "'I will go before you
into Galilee,'" *JTS* 5 (1954) 3-18; J. Schreiber, "Die Christologie des
Markusevangeliums. Beobachtungen zur Theologie und Komposition des
zweiten Evangeliums," *ZTK* 58 (1961) 154-183: "Markus versteht die
Landschaft Galilaa nach Jes 8,23 als das Galilaa der Heiden" (p. 172):
M. Karnetzki, "Die galiläische Redaktion im Markusevangelium," *ZNW* 52
(1961) 238-272; N. Q. Hamilton, "Resurrection Tradition and the Composition of Mark," *JBL* 84 (1965) 415-421.

[29] E. Lohmeyer, *Galilaa und Jerusalem* ("Forschungen zur Religion und
Literatur des Alten und Neuen Testaments," N.F. 34; Göttingen, 1936);
W. Marxsen, *Der Evangelist Markus* (Göttingen, 1956) 60.

[30] For example, E. P. Gould, *A Critical and Exegetical Commentary on the Gospel according to St. Mark* ("International Critical Commentary"; Edinburgh, 1897) xvii: Rome, just before 70; B. Weiss, *Die Evangelien des Markus und Lukas* (9th ed. rev.; "Kritisch-exegetischer Kommentar über das Neue Testament"; Göttingen, 1901) 9-10: Rome, before 70; H. B. Swete, *The Gospel according to St. Mark* (2nd ed.; London, 1908) xxxix-xl: Rome, before 70; G. Wohlenberg, *Das Evangelium des Markus* (Leipzig, 1910) 24-29: Rome, around 67; A. E. J. Rawlinson, *The Gospel according to St. Mark* (4th ed.; "Westminster Commentaries"; London, 1936) xxiv-xxxi: Rome, around 65-67; B. H. Branscomb, *The Gospel of Mark* ("Moffatt NT Commentary"; London, 1937) xv-xviii, xxix-xxxi: Rome, around 75; F. C. Grant, "The Gospel according to St. Mark," *The Interpreter's Bible* VII (New York, 1951) 630: Rome, before 70, "writing for a martyr church"; W. Grundmann, *Das Evangelium nach Markus* (2nd ed. rev.; "Theologischer Handkommentar zum NT"; Berlin, 1959) 18-19: Rome, between 62 and 69; S. E. Johnson, *The Gospel according to St. Mark* ("Black's NT Commentaries"; London, 1960) 14-20: Rome, during 71-73; C. E. B. Cranfield, *The Gospel according to St. Mark* (Cambridge, 1963) 8-9: Rome, in 65-67: V. Taylor, *The Gospel according to St. Mark* (2nd ed.; London, 1966) 31-32: Rome ("much stronger"), during 60-70 ("generally agreed"); S. G. F. Brandon, "The Date of the Markan Gospel," *NTS* 7 (1960-1) 126-141 who argues for Rome after the Flavian triumph in 71 states: "According to the general consensus of expert opinion the Gospel of Mark was composed sometime between the years A.D. 65-75" (p. 127).

[31] A. George, "Le sens de la parabole des semailles (Mc., IV,3-9 et parallèles)," *Sacra Pagina. Miscellanea Biblica Congressus Internationalis Catholici de Re Biblica* ("Bibliotheca ETL," 13; Gembloux, 1959) II, 163-169.

[32] The *meta diōgmōn* of Mk 10,30 has no parallel in Mt 19,29 and Lk 18,30. Its addition in 10,30 and the consequent necessity of omitting one member from 10,29 to preserve the seven-fold list in both draws special attention to Mark's use of the phrase.

[33] The basis for this transition during a reversed journey may well be the event of 2 Kg 2 in which the mantle of Elijah passes to Elisha at the turning point of a journey from north to south (2,1-8) and back north again (2,13-25).